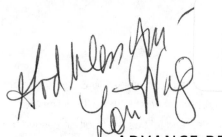

ADVANCE PRAISE FOR

GENDER & MINISTRY

I have met two sorts of people who don't believe in women ministers: those who simply have not met a woman effective in ministry and those who have biblical questions; specifically, questions as to whether the Bible prohibits a woman from pulpit ministry. In *Gender & Ministry*, Lori Wagner, a dynamic woman minister, tackles the subject head on, conversing with accepted scholars in the field. She digs deeply into the most relevant passages, even those difficult passages which, on the face of it, seem to be restrictive to women. I recommend this excellent study for any serious student of the Bible. It belongs in your library.

—David S. Norris, PhD
  Professor of Biblical Theology
  Urshan Graduate School of Theology

Gender and ministry is a daunting topic anytime but, in these times, it is more complex than ever before. Identifying, approaching, and confronting the sensitive issue of women in ministry requires a special skill set. Lori Wagner has accomplished the three challenges and her God-given skill set has provided an incredible pathway through the maze of complications. I strongly urge every minister, both men and women, to thoroughly and thoughtfully consider her insight and wisdom. Open your heart, open the Word and open your arms to the army of women who have the capacity to change the world.

—Janet Trout, Chair
  Board of Directors
  Urshan College and Urshan Graduate School of Theology

Lori Wagner has written a carefully researched study. In *Gender & Ministry* she covers biblical examples of women in spiritual leadership throughout the Old Testament, examines New Testament examples, and follows the tradition beyond the apostolic age into church history. Wagner offers several possible explanations for the few passages that appear to suggest that women should not be used in leadership, and gives the reader avenues for additional research with several pages of bibliography and endnotes. By examining the scriptures as a whole, Wagner successfully refutes the proof-texting commonly used against women in ministry and affirms both those women who are called to the ministry and the men who support them. I highly recommend this book to anyone with questions regarding women in ministry!

—Mitchell McQuinn, MTS (ABT)
   Pastor, Sudbury, Ontario

Lori Wagner is not a novice when it comes to putting pen to paper. Her passion for God, her calling, and her ministry are evident in each project she tackles. *Gender & Ministry* is no exception. Lori lives this subject and represents it to its fullest extent.

—Lois Mitchell
   Chair, Women in Ministry Network

Thank you, Lori Wagner, for making a strong scriptural declaration of God's plan for women in His church by writing *Gender & Ministry*. Thank you also for setting an example for women to be humble, faithful, and yielded to the Lord.

—Daniel Koren
   Pastor & Author of *He Called Her*

GENDER
AND
MINISTRY

A Biblical and Historical Investigation of Women in Ministry

LORI WAGNER

AFFIRMING FAITH
Clarkston, Michigan

AFFIRMING FAITH
8900 Ortonville Road | Clarkston, MI 48348 | www.affirmingfaith.org

Printed in the United States of America | Design: Laura Merchant

Library of Congress Cataloging-in-Publication Data
Names: Wagner, Lori, 1965 – author.
Title: Gender and Ministry / Lori Wagner
Description: Clarkston : Affirming Faith. | Includes bibliographical references. | Includes index.
Identifiers: LCCN 2018902865 | ISBN 978-0-9897373-6-4 (paperback)
Subjects: LCSH: Women clergy. | Women in Christianity—History. | Women in Church Work—History. | Sex role—Religious aspects. | Christian women—Religious life.

Dedication

This book is dedicated to Bill Wagner.

Thank you, my amazing husband, for your unending, selfless, support.
Wherever I go, I take your name.
Whatever I write, your name is next to mine.
We are one. I love you.

Acknowledgements

A book may have one name on its cover, but it's never entirely the work of one person. In the case of *Gender & Ministry*, years of teaching and inspiration from countless ministers, colleagues, and friends have contributed to the work you now hold in your hands.

My first and deepest thanks go to the Giver of every good gift—which includes the gift of writing. Thank you, Jesus, the Author and Finisher of my faith, for pressing me with this project and helping me every step along the way to its completion. Secondly, I honor and thank my husband, Bill Wagner, and my family who have faithfully, lovingly stood beside me through the many ups and downs of writing and ministry.

I would like to express my sincere gratitude to all who gave input, guidance, or written contributions. Some offered listening ears that helped me talk things out. Others gave expertise and information that helped me figure things out. While many names are noted in the book, I would like to particularly thank Dr. David K. Bernard, Rev. Daniel Koren, and Rev. Gwyn Oakes.

Warm thanks to Rev. Marvin and Claudette Walker. Their pastoral blessings and continuous support have inspired me to keep moving forward as the Lord lights the way.

I appreciate the incredible help I received from my editor, Kent Curry, and the additional editorial assistance provided by Dr. Beth Jan Smith. Thanks to Rev. Carla Gray Weiser for sharing her research study on women in ministry and to Crystal A. Napier, Archivist at the Center for the Study of Oneness Pentecostalism, for her assistance plowing through historical documents.

Lastly, I want to thank every person who shared a kind word or faithfully prayed for this project and its writer. God only knows what your support meant to me and the impact you made on this book. God bless each one of you.

Contents

Foreword

From youth, women involved in ministry impacted my life. As an adolescent, I was pastored by the Caughrons. Sis. Caughron was a more effective evangelistic preacher than her husband. As an evangelist, I preached for Hazel Simpson who raised up a strong church in Millington, Tennessee. I have been blessed by the pulpit ministry of women like Bobbye Wendell and Vesta Mangun; and Janet Trout served as an effective district leader for North American Missions.

Women have made and are making a difference in the kingdom of God. Even now, some women are establishing churches in places where otherwise we simply would not have a church. Neglecting to empower both men and women for meaningful ministry would be a waste. Yes, we need preachers—preachers who will go and do. Men and women are needed.

Success and a history of effectiveness would seem to nullify the question of women in ministry, but for those still looking for clarity on the biblical basis for women in the pulpit or in church leadership, I recommend Lori Wagner's *Gender & Ministry*. "In Christ there is neither male nor female," and at times the voice of an anointed woman breaks through barriers a man has not accomplished.

—Rev. Carlton L. Coon, Sr.
Pastor, Author, and Former Director—North American Missions (UPCI)

Introduction

I n 2017, Affirming Faith published *Preach Like a Lady* to encourage and equip women called to Christian ministry. The handbook earned superlative reviews from ministry-minded women, as well as church leaders and educators. The second part of the book, an extensive biblical and historical investigation of women in ministry, has been updated for a general readership and offered now as a stand-alone work, *Gender & Ministry*. This resource is suitable for anyone, male or female, interested in learning more on the subject of women in ministry but who would not benefit from the full text of the original ministerial handbook.

Throughout *Gender & Ministry,* readers will notice the absence of terms like "equality," "rights," and "biblical feminism" commonly used in civil rights conversations. Jesus set the example for his church and its leaders. Ministry is serving and should never be degraded by anyone demanding rights or attempting to dominate others. Followers of Jesus should, however, seek to understand the Lord's true intentions for his daughters, which may or may not align with modern cultural or church paradigms.

Careful students of Scripture understand that individual doctrinal viewpoints must agree with the whole Word of God. With that in mind, it's my prayer readers consider this work unskewed by lenses of tradition or personal belief systems and instead strive to find God's heart on the matter. What was his purpose in creating woman? What happened to that purpose at the fall, at the cross, and in the upper room? And how do the answers to these questions impact the roles women may serve in the Lord's church today?

Lori Wagner

In the Beginning

So God created man in his own image, in the image of God created he him; male and female created he them.
Genesis 1:27

"In the beginning, God created...."

These powerful words established the record of God's original design for humanity.

The creation of mankind is introduced in the first book of the Bible in two parallel verses: Genesis 1:26 and 1:27. Biblical writers utilized parallel verses to strengthen a point they were making. The complete meaning of both verses is not understood in one verse or the other, but both verses together deliver the complete meaning.[1] When a writer utilized parallel verses, "Verse A" and "Verse B" were not meant to be treated as independent statements even if their structures formed grammatically complete sentences.

As you read Genesis 1:26–27 below, bear in mind these two verses form one complete thought—the second verse strengthening and adding more information to the first.

"And God said, Let us make man in our image, after our likeness: and let them have dominion over the fish of the sea, and over the fowl of the air, and over the cattle, and over all the earth, and over every creeping thing that creepeth upon the earth. So God created man in his own image, in the image of God created he him; male and female created he them."

This couplet reveals God's original plan in making mankind—to be like him. Both male and female were made in his image and both were given dominion over all the earth. In Genesis 1:27, the word "man" translated from the Hebrew word 'adam refers to "humankind" which comes in two forms, male and female. Both are made in the image of God. Neither alone bears his full image.

The "image of God" indicates resemblance, like a shadow. Since God is a Spirit,[2] he has no physical body. Therefore, we shouldn't consider his "being" in relation to the physical bodies of human beings. Instead, God's image refers to the spirit nature he created in Adam and Eve. As spiritual beings, the Lord made humans to function as his representatives, doing the work he gave them of ruling over the earth and creating life in earth. They worked together—one complementing the other to fulfill the purposes of God.

Our Creator is neither male nor female. The Lord is a spirit, and his essence is reflected in the joint creation of male and female. Although pronouns like "him" and "his" are used by people to communicate about God, the Lord has no gender identity and should not be considered masculine based on a biblical usage of gender-specific pronouns. In fact, the Word talks about God's arms, eyes, hands, wings, and breasts, among other anatomical terms. Before the birth of Jesus, the Spirit of God had no physical body, so how can these anatomical terms apply? There must be additional information to consider.

"Our Father, which art in heaven" is more than just our Father. Scripture calls the Lord "husband" (see Isa 54:5). The same "being" as father and husband can only be rationalized when the Word is approached with the understanding that each description of God reveals a different facet of his nature, his character, or humanity's relationship with him.

It has been said the image of God is a "double image" that transcends gender and has both masculine and feminine characteristics. The Lord "bore" his people like a mother bears a child (see Deut 32:18). He likened the way he comforted his people to a mother comforting her child, and a mother hen gathering her chicks (see Isa 66:13; Matt 23:37).

In Genesis 1, Scripture tells us that Adam was made from the dust of the ground and given the breath of life from God. In the second chapter of Genesis, the Bible flashes back and zooms in on the sixth day of creation. Genesis 1:27 provided an overview. In Genesis 2:18, God revealed an important detail. Up to this point, everything he had made he deemed good, but in verse 18, he said it was *not* good for Adam to be alone. He recognized the longing in Adam's heart, his feelings of "incompleteness" even while living in paradise, and the Lord determined to make him a "help meet." Creation without woman was not good. It was incomplete.

"And the Lord God caused a deep sleep to fall upon Adam, and he slept: and he took one of his ribs, and closed up the flesh instead thereof; And the rib, which the Lord God had taken from man, made he a woman, and brought her unto the man" (Gen 2:21–22).

I believe God knew the longing Adam had because it was an experience he shared with him. The Lord had no one of his kind, no one "like" him, so he decided to make one. The Lord scooped up dirt and made Adam and then Eve from the same building materials—all with an end-goal in view, his bride.

Understanding "Help Meet"

The order of creation never implies a lesser value, capability, or an authoritative hierarchy (a system of ranking one person above another). The question, however, is still out for many: What exactly is a "help meet?" Does the use of this word indicate Eve was "subordinate," "suitable," or "similar" to Adam?

The term "help meet" is rendered from two Hebrew words. The first is `ezer, which means "aid" and "help." It comes from a root word that's "primary idea lies in girding, surrounding, hence defending."[3] These meanings certainly do not imply weakness, but rather strength. In fact, the Lord calls himself Israel's `ezer in Scripture (see Hos 13:9). He is the help that comes from the hills and the shield about his people (see Ps 121:1; Deut 33:29; Ps 33:20). He was their military ally. Certainly no one would propose that when the Lord was identified as Israel's helper he was subordinate or under Israel's authority.

The second Hebrew word *neged* translated "meet" brings additional clarity to this compound description of woman. It means "the front part" and "as over against" which implies things that are alike but are being compared. Specifically, in reference to Genesis 1:27, the meaning of *neged* is "corresponding to him." In rabbinical teaching the word *neged* was often used "in speaking of things which are like one another."[4] Eve was created by God for a face-to-face relationship with Adam.

Adam looked into Eve's face and saw the image of God. Eve looked into Adam's face and saw the same.

When Adam first identified Eve in verse 23, he did not give her a proper name, but designated her "kind" and gender. Similar to the way "tigress" is the feminine of tiger, woman is the feminine form of man.

The use of the word *neged* implies Eve was Adam's spiritual and intellectual equal. She was made of the same substance and essence. She was created to be a strength, help, and blessing, and God placed her right in front of Adam—a "help corresponding to him i.e. equal and adequate to himself."[5] The *Septuagint* (a Koine Greek translation of the Old Testament from the Hebrew Scriptures used widely by the Jews dispersed through the Roman Empire) translates the "helper" Adam could not find in Genesis 2:20 as the Greek word *homoios*.[6] This word means "like, resembling, similar"[7] and signifies equality. In addition, *homoios* not only relates to appearance and form, but "of ability, condition, nature," as well as like in "action, thought."[8]

The Lord presented Eve to Adam in the Garden to transform his "not good" to "very good." She was his friend, lover, and partner. The first couple shared in divine origin, sacred purpose, failure, and prophetic hope.

Adam was overjoyed when he met the flesh of his flesh and bone of his bone. In a sense, he was meeting part of himself repackaged into a similar and corresponding mate—one of his own kind who was neither inferior nor superior. In fact, mankind's first recorded words are found in Adam's loving response to Eve. "This is now bone of my bones, and flesh of my flesh: she shall be called Woman, because she was taken out of Man. Therefore shall a man leave his father and his mother, and shall cleave unto his wife: and they shall be one flesh" (Gen 2:23–24).

God made Adam from the dust of the earth, but then fashioned Eve from his substance. He took the "she" out of "he," separating his image into two distinct beings. Although they were created at different times, they were not truly separate creations, but distinct renderings of the same Creator who has feminine, masculine, and gender-neutral attributes.

Yes, the creation account gives a chronological order of formation, but before the fall in a sinless environment, the Bible does not record a governmental hierarchy. Adam and Eve depended on each other to fulfill the will of God. The Lord gave the man and the woman identical charges—to be fruitful and have dominion. These plural commands were given to both Adam and Eve, who were commissioned to lead and govern the earth side by side.

The Fall

The book of Genesis, although it contains a wealth of knowledge, does not give information "before the beginning." When Adam and Eve came on the scene, the devil was already there. From a human perspective, life could have been easier without the devil on location. But God had his purposes.

In the Garden the Lord planted a tree and told man not to eat from it. Some have questioned why he would do such a thing. Perhaps he placed the tree in the Garden as a reminder of who he was and always would be. He gave mankind authority and dominion, but he wanted them to remember he would remain Sovereign over all.

When Satan approached Eve in the Garden, he made her a poor offer. She and Adam were already reigning together. They already had dominion. They were already like God in essence—created in his image. They already had knowledge of good. What Satan misrepresented as an opportunity for more was actually an offer to know evil.

It is important to note that according to the text Eve and Satan were not the only two on the scene at the time she ate the fruit. Eve "took of the fruit thereof, and did eat, and gave also unto her husband with her; and he did eat" (see Gen 3:6). Scripture seems to indicate Adam was in the Garden during the exchange, but Satan spoke to Eve instead of her husband.

Some have proposed Eve was more vulnerable to temptation than Adam. If that were true, it would seem to be a faulty premise to attribute any alleged weakness to her make-up. Eve was made of the same substance as her husband. If Adam had not wanted what the serpent offered, he would have intervened. Consider that God directly gave Adam the prohibition to refrain from eating from the tree before Eve was created (see Gen 2:16). His instruction was apparently transmitted to Eve second-hand. I would propose that if there was a greater weakness in Eve (a point that could be argued either way), her vulnerability could be attributed to her lack of first-hand knowledge of God's words regarding the tree. The fault may well lay in her education, not essential nature; in a failed communication, not a frail, feminine character.

Addressing the Issue

When discussing the dialogue that followed the fall, it's important to remember that God was aware of everything that had happened. He knew all the details, but when he entered the garden, he called for Adam (see Gen 3:9). Adam, in response, turned the Lord's attention to his wife (see Gen 3:12), after which God directly addressed Eve.

This is an interesting occurrence in light of how life played out in the centuries that followed. By the time Jesus was born, a woman was not allowed to testify or speak on her own behalf. But in the Garden, God (knowing the woman had failed) addressed Eve directly. Adam did not speak for her—in fact, he blamed her in an attempt to deflect God away from him. In the Bible, however, we find no record of Eve being held accountable by God for the fall. In fact, the apostle Paul repeated several times that one person was responsible, and in two places identified Adam as the one who led the human race into sin (see Rom 5:14; 1 Tim 2:14).

Some would withhold ministry and leadership opportunities for women in the church on the basis of Eve's failure, but Adam failed as well.

Consequences of the Fall

Curses. God issued two of them after the fall: one on the earth and one on Satan. Adam was not cursed. Eve was not cursed. Cursing implies a loathing that was not in the heart of God for his people. Disobeying the Word, however, brought severe consequences to humanity.

The curses issued in Genesis disturbed the condition of the earth and the standing of the devil who had presented himself in the Garden as a serpent. The serpent was identified as "more subtil than any beast of the field" (see Gen 3:1). The word subtil means "shrewd," "crafty," "sly," "sensible," and "prudent." Many commentary writers support the position that before the fall serpents were some form of erect creature. The serpent after the fall was "cursed above all cattle, and above every beast of the field" (see Gen 3:14). The Lord said, "Upon thy belly shalt thou go, and dust shalt thou eat all the days of thy life" (see Gen 3:14).

Mankind had been created from the dust of the earth, and as the result of sin, the dust of the earth they would become again. Satan would slither in the dust on his belly at the feet of men and women. Even more significantly, the ultimate defeat of Satan would come through the offspring of the woman he deceived. Jesus, the seed of Eve, would bruise the serpent's head and the serpent would "bruise his heel" (see Gen 3:15).

Banished from Eden, Adam and Eve were about to experience a new, foreign way of life. The Lord addressed Eve first with her consequences. "Unto the woman he said, I will greatly multiply thy sorrow and thy conception; in sorrow thou shalt bring forth children" (see Gen 3:16.) Eve would now suffer in childbearing.

Eve's second consequence affected her relationship with her husband. The King James Version translates it this way: "And thy desire *shall be* to thy husband, and he shall rule over thee" (see Gen 3:16). Note God did not vilify Eve, but defined the results of her sin. From that time forward she would live in a world that would be home to both the creation of God and the penalty of sin.

It might be important to note that "shall be" in the above verse is italicized, which means it is not in the original text. Eve's desire to Adam doesn't appear to be the result of a command of God, but again, a result of sin. This statement could well have been prophetic in nature and was certainly fulfilled. *Young's Literal Translation* renders this portion of the verse: "and toward thy husband [is] thy desire, and he doth rule over thee."

As a consequence of the fall Adam and Eve's relationship shifted. Eve would from thereafter have an increased longing for her husband. A reflection of this increased longing can be seen in the way women often turn to men for affirmation and value. Some women are overly dependent on men. This could be a characteristic of woman's fallen nature, but it does not appear to be her created, original nature.

The last of the Lord's words to Eve were, "And he shall rule over thee." The word translated "rule" is the Greek word *mashal*. It has several meanings. Its first use is found in reference to the sun ruling the day and the moon ruling the night (see Gen 1:16). Abraham had a servant who ruled over all he had (see Gen 24:2). Joseph was a ruler in Egypt (see Gen 45:26). To rule can certainly mean to have dominion, but it also has a gentler side. The sun rules the day, but it provides life-giving light to the world. A steward's role, like that of Abraham's steward or Joseph as governor, was to take good care of someone else's possessions for the benefit of others. This brings to mind the words of the Lord in 2 Samuel 23:3, "He that ruleth over men must be just, ruling in the fear of God."

From the beginning, one of the strongest elements of humanity's fallen nature has been the struggle for control. God's original intention was not a patriarchal order, but that a man would leave his father and mother and cleave to his wife.

Proponents of patriarchy *ad infinitum* often cite creation order as evidence of male supremacy, but this simply does not reconcile with Scripture. Some claim Adam "naming" Eve shows his authority over her, but he did not give her the name *Chavvah* (translated Eve) until after the fall. He merely called her "woman." *Chavvah* means "life" or "living" and comes from a root word that means "to breathe." The fact that Eve's name was given to her *after* the fall brings a heightened significance to its meaning. In the face of their judgment for sin and impending deaths, Adam gave his wife a name that held a prophetic meaning. Life and breath would come through his beloved. Humanity would continue and victory would come (see 1 Cor 15:54).

> The "governorship" of a husband over his wife (not all men over all women) is a result of the fall. The husband/wife conflict was not God's original plan, and a Christian man should never "lord over" his wife, especially when she has a longing for his affection and approval.

If naming a person indicates rulership of the person named, the fact that Eve named Seth should be considered (see Gen 4:25). Rachel and Leah named the tribes of Israel. Jacob overrode Rachel in her chosen name for their son Benjamin, but 11 out of 12 is quite a record. Before Joseph learned of Mary's pregnancy, the angel of the Lord told her to name the baby Jesus.

In today's world, men and women continue to suffer the effects of the fall—spiritually and physically. Although in many nations women participate in society and government, men have more often than not ruled and dominated, even in Christian circles. But is this the way the body of Christ should conduct itself? Did the after-the-fall condition of the husband/wife relationship establish male rulership and dominance in society at large and in the church for all time? Should the status of Christian women in the church be based on the post-fall consequences of sin or on the atoning work of Jesus?

Restored by Christ

For as in Adam all die, even so in Christ shall all be made alive.
1 Corinthians 15:22

God's creation undoubtedly suffered the effects of mankind's fall, but did its failure forever alter his intentions for humanity? Did the disobedience of Adam and Eve intrinsically change the Lord's purpose that men and women, united together, would bear his image in the world? Undoubtedly, the glory of God was stripped away, revealing mankind's nakedness, but consider the words of the wisest man on earth, "Whatsoever God doeth, it shall be for ever: nothing can be put to it, nor any thing taken from it" (Ecc 3:14).

The blood of Jesus did a mighty work at Calvary. Through Christ the world was offered salvation, but not all respond to the opportunity. Whoever accepts the Lord's gracious gift, however, becomes a joint heir of Christ and partaker of the reversal of the fall's spiritual effects.

Born again believers no longer live under the repercussions of disobedience. The righteousness of Jesus makes them new creatures and brings them into a new spiritual realm. Yes, mankind still lives in a fallen world, but within the church redemption reigns. *Logos*, the very plan of God, became redemption and brought redemption. The power of grace is that it brings restoration of what was lost. Mankind's loving Father did not abandon his children to the consequences of sin.

The work of the cross set humanity free from the curse of the law and offers liberty and restoration to those who believe. In Christ all things can be made new. Jesus restores. Jesus renames. Jesus resurrects.

Some glad morning there will be a restoration of "all things" (see Acts 3:21). Meanwhile, for believers, what was wasted spiritually in Eden is now restored. Paul wrote

Romans 8:20–21 to let Christ-followers know that while there is sin, death, and decay in the world, these curses will someday disappear altogether. The world is in a process of yielding to the will of God, and it will one day join in glorious freedom from sin.

But how does this apply to the role of women in ministry in the church today? Did the blood of Jesus provide the opportunity for all to be restored to a pre-fall condition in relationship with God? In relationship with other believers? Did not Christ redeem humanity and set believers free from both the constraining power of sin and their corrupt natures?

For those who are in Christ, sin no longer dominates. Believers are restored. They not only have access to God but have God-given authority to serve as his priests and ambassadors in the community of his reconciled people. Outside the church darkness and sin promenade with the prince of this world, but God's people are part of a new covenant.

Jesus came to earth on a mission—to restore abundant life (see John 10:10). He imparted his righteousness and divine nature into sinful, fallen lives. As the first Adam represented all humanity in the fall; Jesus, the last Adam, represented all humanity on the cross. Through his sacrifice the very life and nature of God were imparted back into the world (see 1 Cor 15:45).

The Lord implanted his redemption plan into the womb of a "daughter of Eve." In his flesh Jesus abolished the hostility between Jews and Gentiles (see Eph 2:16). He brought two opposite peoples together and made them one. This harmonizes with Galatians 3:28 that proclaims in Christ there are no divisions, "There is neither Jew nor Greek, there is neither bond nor free, there is neither male nor female: for ye are all one in Christ Jesus." Through his sacrificial death, Jesus removed the partitions for all, allowing equal access to every believer to the presence of God, the family of God, and the service of God (see Eph 2:14).

The Power of Pentecost

Jesus accepted women as disciples, and this precedent continued with his followers after his death, burial, and resurrection. Before and after his ascension, both men and women were baptized as part of their new birth experiences. This was incredibly significant, because in the old covenant only men could be circumcised, and circumcision was the outward sign of covenant with God. Through baptism women experienced the "circumcision made without hands" (see Col 2:11–12) and the infilling of the Spirit gave them full membership and participation in the church (see Acts 2:38).

In the upper room both men and women received the gift of the Holy Spirit and individually acquired the power of God in their lives (see Acts 2:4). Every person present spoke divine utterances and extolled the wonders of God among the people. It was the dawn of a new age, the church age, and it changed the world forever.

On that day, as men and women from all stations of life and nationalities heard the believers speaking in tongues and the message of salvation in Christ, their hearts were pricked. Joel had prophesied it, and the Lord fulfilled his promise. He poured out his Spirit upon all flesh, and the sons and daughters prophesied (see Joel 2:28).

Not only was the fulfillment of this "all flesh" promise significant to women, it opened the door to Gentiles. With the outpouring of the Holy Spirit every perceived hindrance was stripped away and mankind entered an age in which every person could access God for him or herself regardless of race, gender, or social status. It was what they had been waiting for—what Jesus had promised would empower them to be his witnesses.

The fact that every man and woman received the Holy Spirit evidenced God's intention that all believers should participate in the Great Commission—one of the main reasons the Lord gave for receiving divine empowerment. To further bolster this point, notice how the outpouring happened on the only Jewish feast day women were required to attend (see Deut 16:1–15). Jewish women were not commanded to participate in other feast days (see Deut 16:16). On this day of celebration, however, women followers of Jesus assembled with the men in the upper room, and in the streets of Jerusalem women would have been among those who heard the Spirit-filled believers preach the good news of salvation by Christ Jesus.

Following the outpouring of the spirit of God on the day of Pentecost, ministry roles in the infant church took a dynamic shift from a priestly Judaic hierarchy to a new form of government. Scripture mentions many women by name, including Dorcas and Lydia, as disciples and followers of Christ. Many women (including the mother of Jesus) remained with Jesus's disciples after the Lord's ascension, and they devoted themselves to prayer (see Acts 1:14).

Women took part in coed services alongside men. In addition, the Bible mentions the presence of many "chief women" and many honorable Greek women (see Acts 17:4, 17:12). A reading through the book of Acts and the Epistles lets us know churches met predominantly in women's homes and most likely under their leadership.

2 — *Restored by Christ*

Further reading in the book of Acts reveals that although Peter received the Holy Spirit and preached the incredible message on the day of Pentecost, he lacked revelation about the magnitude of what God had done. Oddly enough, this man who had no lineage or education—this fisherman turned apostle by the grace of God—held to some prejudices the Lord had to deal with by sending him a special vision (see Acts 10:9-16). As a result of this spiritual encounter, Peter received revelation of God's plan to include the Gentiles in salvation. His concepts and ministry transformed and he became a minister and advocate for receiving Gentiles as fellow members of the New Testament church.

Like Peter, contemporary believers should be willing to evaluate their perception of ministry roles in the church to determine if they are based on God's intentions or accepted cultural norms. God is no respecter of persons. There may be those who, like Peter, have not offered all their preconceptions to the Lord. Our church and ministry paradigms should agree with God's revealed plan and the whole counsel of his Word.

Some confusion may lie in a faulty misapplication of the role of the Old Testament priesthood to the structure of the New Testament ministry, but the old model was never God's plan. It could be that a few intentionally corrupted God's plan for personal gain and power and what they established as norms have been accepted by God-fearing people in the church at large. But the Lord was careful to teach his believers not to lord one over another. In fact, he was very clear when he gave a counter-culture directive to his disciples in regards to their call to leadership: "It shall not be so among you" (see Matt 20:26).

In the early church, preaching was not relegated only to men, but women also preached. As believers everywhere continue to receive the gift of the Spirit, sinners become saints. Individuals are restored spiritually to a pre-fall condition with God. Both men and women have direct access to the throne of God. The curse of sin is broken, and believers become part of one body. In Christ—in the spirit-realm—gender is no longer relevant; and a caste ranking of humanity simply does not apply.

In Christ

The body of Christ is a unique spiritual organism composed of men and women from all ethnicities and social stratum. The Word gives a picture of heaven in which the redeemed includes "every kindred, and tongue, and people, and nation" (see Rev 5:8).

In Christ, Jews and non-Jews had access to the righteousness of God. It sprang from faith and led believers into more faith (see Rom 1:16–8). As faith grows, believers have clearer insights into the righteousness of God. Paul, the writer of Galatians, Romans, Timothy, and Corinthians certainly experienced the transforming power that leads from "faith to faith" (see Acts 9).

As a Pharisee, Paul (when he was known as Saul) would likely have started his morning with the prayer recited daily by devout Jewish men. According to Rabbi Judah bar Ilai (the second-century sage most frequently mentioned in the *Mishna*, ancient rabbinic literature), the following benedictions were recited by Jewish men every day:

Paul (who wrote passages some believe restrict women from ministry) authored a pivotal verse of Scripture: "There is neither Jew nor Greek, there is neither slave nor free, there is neither male nor female; for you are all one in Christ Jesus" (Gal 3:28). Any perceived restrictions written by Paul elsewhere must harmonize with this passage that clearly expresses the basic composition and function of the church. All are one.

1. Blessed be he who did not make me a Gentile.
2. Blessed be he who did not make me a woman.
3. Blessed be he who did not make me an uneducated man (bondman or slave).

Imagine the hopeless state for women. Gentile men could be circumcised and accepted as converts to Judaism. Slaves could earn or be given their freedom. But a woman had no hope of ever "bettering" her station in life.

The good news of the gospel contains the good word that in Christ, racial, gender, and social differences are irrelevant. They are transcended. This concept does not negate the family structure, but affirms that women in the body of Christ have equal access and opportunity to a relationship with God and function in ministry. This overturned hundreds of years of social history in every major culture. What we assume is ordinary is actually ordinary because it was extraordinary.

Could it be that in writing to the Galatians Paul expressly identified the three categories the daily Jewish prayer demeaned as subordinate in rank to the basest male Jew (Gentiles, slaves, and females)? "There is neither Jew nor Greek, bond nor free, male nor female." Was Paul revealing to this new community of believers that discrepancies held in Judaism no longer applied in the church of Jesus Christ?

> The concept of parity in the function of the members of the body reflects back to Eden and forward to heaven. In the Spirit-filled church of God, gender is no criteria to serve the Lord.

This passage in Galatians acknowledges the reality of distinctions in gender, ethnicity, and social standing. In Paul's day, there was also the legal standing of free and slave. Paul reiterated his Galatians 3:28 statement in Colossians when he spoke of the unity within the church. For those who "put on the new man ... there is neither Greek nor Jew, circumcision nor uncircumcision, Barbarian, Scythian, bond nor free: but Christ is all, and in all" (Col 3:10–11).

These passages are important to anyone who might be discriminated against. Imagine these scenarios in the first century church:

- Slaves hear Paul declare spiritual emancipation in Christ.
- Gentiles receive the revelation that God would accept them regardless of their bloodline and without adhering to all the Jewish ceremonial law and rites.
- Women are given a public voice and allowed to function in the congregation of believers.

When evaluating Paul's words, remember the apostle was dealing with relationships within the church that did not align with the customs of his contemporary secular or Jewish society. For instance, slavery was a common practice, but in the assembly of believers a slave was free to be a fully participating member.

In Christ any differences recognized elsewhere should not have impacted a believer's position or practice in the church.

In North America today, discrimination based on a person's race is not tolerated. And in the body of Christ also, the color of a believer's skin should neither elevate nor bar a person from ministry roles. Ideally, this same freedom should be enjoyed by every member of the church. Every Christian is of equal value, and that value is the price paid to redeem them. Each individual believer holds the same position before God—a sinner redeemed by the blood of Jesus Christ. Allowing for differences in individual giftings and callings, equal footing at the foot of the cross should mean equal access to ministry functions in the church.

In Paul's letters he addressed the churches "as they were," while he held up a standard of "this is what you should be." The early church came with a lot of baggage from strict religious orthodoxy to paganism. Believers were new creatures in Christ, but they were not mature. They were in the process of being discipled and growing in their understanding of the Lord's ways in a culture that was often not on the same page as Christianity.

Paul's declaration "there is neither Jew nor Greek, bond nor free, male nor female" in Galatians is sandwiched between two verses that specify:

1. Who he was referencing (those who had been baptized into Christ), and
2. The result (baptized believers are now in the lineage of Father Abraham and heirs according to God's promise).

As a member of the family of God every believer, male or female, has an inheritance. After all, people simply wear robes of flesh over their eternal souls. Body and soul create one harmonious unit, but one does not define the other. I am not a Caucasion woman. I am a soul, enlivened by the spirit of God, wearing the "garment" of a Caucasion woman. As long as a believer is wearing his or her "wedding garment," they should receive the full benefits of their invitation to be part of the bride of Christ.

First Century Culture and Biblical History

This thing was not done in a corner.
Acts 26:26

To correctly understand the New Testament requires some study of ancient Jewish and Roman history. The following is a brief tour of the land and culture in which Jesus was born.

In 510 BC, ancient Greece emerged from the fall of a tyrannical reign in the fifth and fourth centuries BC. Following the subsequent leadership and death of Alexander the Great, classical Greece entered what is known as the Hellenistic period. The Hellenistic period was a time the Greeks saw great advances in sciences and a transition from Classical Greek philosophies to one that embraced decadence, pleasure-seeking, new gods, and eastern deities. It was at this time Greek influence peaked and spread throughout Europe, Africa, and Asia.

Through a series of wars, Rome emerged as a super power in the second century BC and brought the Hellenistic period to a close when it acquired both Greece and Asia Minor. After a period of instability and unrest, the Roman Empire eventually gained control of the entire Mediterranean basin and several other lands including Germania, Britannia, and Mesopotamia.[9]

A New World

Greek and Roman civilizations interlocked into what became known as the Greco-Roman world. This Mediterranean world was bilingual, with widespread use of Latin and Greek. It was ruled by the Roman Empire with assigned governors and kings to rule on its behalf. Greek philosophies, dress, and entertainments were pervasive in the

Hellenized urban areas of the Empire—the places where Greek ideas and customs were adopted. The Empire, for the most part, was controlled by a small wealthy elite, and there was a huge gap between the "haves" and the "have-nots." The population included a large number of slaves, often taken as the spoils of battle.[10]

At the time of Jesus's birth, the Mediterranean world was in the middle of a long period of relative peacefulness. It was a period called Pax Romana, which is Latin for "Roman Peace." During this 200-year era, the population of the Roman Empire grew to an estimated 70 million people, and the empire experienced unprecedented peace and economic prosperity. Roads were built, commerce was established, and people traveled freely.

Religious philosophies varied greatly and included:
- Dualism (Plato's "two worlds" view)
- Stoicism (Zeno's reason-based philosophy)
- Epicureanism (Epicurus's doctrine of "pleasure is the highest good")
- Gnosticism (ancient heresies that stressed gaining hidden knowledge)
- "Mystery Religions" (secret cults with private initiation ceremonies)
- Judaism (the monotheistic religion of the Jews).[11]

The most influential religion in the first centuries of the Roman Empire involved the "Mystery Religions." In the Greco-Roman world there was no lack of deities. According to their writings, mythological gods and goddesses (the "immortals") were not of human origin. Roman and Greek gods and goddesses were quite similar in nature, but bore different names. For instance, in Roman mythology, Venus was worshipped as the goddess of erotic love, beauty, and fertility; while Greeks venerated Aphrodite for the same reasons.

In a culture that worshiped a goddess who celebrated adultery and prostitution it's no wonder the "goddess of marriage" (Juno for the Romans and Hera for the Greeks) was portrayed as the enemy of the goddess of erotic love. For many, marriage became a duty to carry on the family name, and wives were relegated to lives of obscurity.

Women in the Greco-Roman World

In ancient Rome, freeborn women were considered Roman citizens but they could not vote or hold political office. They held limited public roles, although a few aristocratic women gained some influence.

In Roman culture, it was customary that a woman was not given her own name but was instead called by the feminine form of her father's name.[12] In fact, it was not unusual for sisters to share the same name. When a woman married, she kept her family name but would then become identified in relation to her husband. For instance, a man named Julius might call his daughter Julia. If Julia married Gaius, she would be called, "Julia Gaius," or "Julia [wife] of Gaius."[13]

A woman's religion was a given. In her father's home, she held the faith of her father. When she married, she worshipped according to her husband's beliefs. In a Greek world filled with goddesses, most women found themselves on the opposite side of the "veneration coin." Men generally mistrusted those of the fairer sex. In the Greek account of creation entitled the *Theogony*, Zeus was known as the "allfather." Out of anger, he ordered the creation of the first mortal woman. Her name was Pandora and she was maliciously designed to be both beautiful and evil. When Zeus gave Pandora to Epimetheus (a god formed by the union of heaven and earth, also known as a Titan), Pandora promptly opened and scattered the contents of a jar she brought with her. In so doing she unleashed misery on all mankind. The impetus behind the creation of the first mortal woman according to Greek mythology (revenge) is diametrically opposed to God's loving intention in creating an Eve for his Adam.

In Greek society, women were not to be trusted and had little to say about their destinies. They were on the same legal footing as slaves. They could not receive inheritance or engage in more-than-insignificant domestic business transactions.[14] In fact, women were often not referred to by their own names, but called "the wife of" or "the daughter of."

Demosthenes, a Greek orator and statesman in the fourth century BC, said, "Mistresses we keep for the sake of pleasure, concubines for the daily care of our persons, but wives to bear us legitimate children and to be faithful guardians of our households."[15] In the Greek world, respectable women kept to their homes which were segregated into male and female quarters. Their interaction with men was limited, even at mealtimes.

A Side Trip to Corinth

In addition to understanding the world Jesus entered, recognizing the culture of the Corinthians at the time Paul wrote the church there could make the difference between rightly dividing or misapplying Scripture relevant to the subject of women in ministry. Corinth was a New Testament "sin city," and the apostle had his work cut out for him.

Located at a major crossroads, Corinth had grown to become Greece's greatest city. As we also see in our large metropolises today, the opulence of the rich stood in stark contrast to the deprivation of the poor. The city was the heart and hub of the arts, culture, trade, athletic competitions, and wantonness. It had such a bad reputation, Aristophanes (a fifth century playwright) coined the word *korinthiazethai* in its honor. *Korinthiazethai* is a verb which translates "to act like a Corinthian" and meant "to practice fornication."[16] Plato used the Greek *korinthia kórē,* which translates "Corinthian girl" to mean "prostitute."[17]

The sexual morals of the Corinthians were markedly dissimilar to those observed by Jews and Christians in the first century church. Greek pagans were engrossed in promiscuity and drunkenness. Prostitution was not only a huge factor in their economy, it was a revered practice in pagan worship in many of the city's vast religious cults.

When reading Paul's writings to the Corinthian Christians, consider the challenges he faced planting a church in this pagan environment. In the spiritually young congregation, elements of Corinthian practices would have filtered in through new converts just starting their journey of sanctification. The church was likely made up of members from a broad base of social classes.[18] Racially and culturally, the church was a melting pot—a spiritual nursery to newly converted slaves, Jews, and Gentiles.

In his letters to the Corinthians, Paul stood strong against the prevailing attitudes and ideologies of the Greeks, Romans, and even the Jews in the Mediterranean world. He taught the more excellent way—the better way of love. In the pagan and patriarchal culture that dominated his world and assigned a status of inferiority to women, Paul taught the words and works of Jesus Christ:

- The leveling of all status at the foot of the cross (see Gal 3:26–29)
- The washing away of every barrier by the blood of Jesus Christ (see Eph 1:5–6)
- The regenerating work of the Holy Spirit that made all things new (see 2 Cor 5:17).

Judaism

In the last part of the first century BC, Jewish and Roman cultures began to overlap. The Jews had been dispersed and migrated to Rome, Asia Minor, Babylon, and

Alexandria. In Israel proper, women had a lower role in society, but in other cities of Rome they held more prominent roles. Records have been found from the time of the dispersion that document female elders or rulers of synagogues.[19]

In Israel, women were not provided the opportunity for formal religious education. In fact, they had virtually no legal, social, or economic liberties. They enjoyed little esteem from men and their voices were often restricted and suppressed.

Into This Was Born a Savior

Jesus was born into this segment of the world controlled by the Roman Empire. Born a Jew, he lived in Palestine, which was a part of the Roman Empire. It was a pluralistic world—an assortment of ethnicities, ranking officials, merchants, slaves, and minorities. In this time of peace, people of diverse religions were allowed to worship in the Empire according to their beliefs but under strict Roman authority and governorship.

Understanding the political, social, cultural, and religious values and beliefs of the people of Jesus's day helps believers today understand the magnitude of the Lord's words and actions. They were in high contrast to the world in which he lived. For women of the day—especially intelligent, gifted, and spiritually motivated women—this Gentile-Jewish world could well have been a disheartening place. Perhaps that is why so many women responded with adoration to the Savior and his gospel that offered them freedom they were forbidden elsewhere.

Biblical History

When Jesus began his earthly ministry the wheels of change creaked and moaned before they rolled out of the ruts of some comfortable old paths. Although not everyone wanted to be steered into new ways of thinking, the Messiah came to bring change. Jesus was revolutionary. He turned many of the standard practices of his day completely upside down. In the gospels, themes replay. For instance, Jesus said more than once, "You have heard it said," followed by, "but I say to you."

Jesus built upon former teachings. He called people to live by higher standards of morality and spirituality than they had previously known. Other times he redirected their ways of living and worshipping back to "in the beginning it was not so." Jesus addressed controversial issues like polygamy, adultery, divorce, revenge, and even giving money to religious causes. His interaction with women was revolutionary, as well.

In his teaching, Jesus used women over and again as examples to reveal spiritual truths. His parables included women kneading bread, searching for a lost coin, petitioning an unjust judge, giving sacrificially, and serving as bridesmaids. Three of these parables were direct comparisons to the kingdom of God.

Jesus was not gender prejudiced, but gender impartial. From the manger to the sermon on the mount, from his crucifixion to that glorious resurrection morning, women were a part of the life and ministry of the Messiah. When Jesus spoke, he purposely used inclusive language. Many places in Scripture where translators chose the word "man" to identify who he was addressing or teaching, the Lord's language could be more accurately rendered "human" or "person." His use of the term "daughter of Abraham" was unprecedented (see Luke 13:16).

Mary and Martha

When Jesus taught in public places like the hillsides and in the villages, he opened his ministry to women in a new way. Teaching was offered to men in the temple and synagogues, but Jesus taught everywhere in both public and private settings. It was in Martha's home Jesus affirmed a woman's right to learn. When Martha spoke to Jesus about her sister Mary's lack of support with food preparation, he said Mary had "chosen that good part, which shall not be taken away from her" (see Luke 10:42). Jesus didn't reprimand Mary for choosing learning over "women's work." He commended her. This scenario provided the perfect opportunity for Jesus to settle the question of women learning once and for all, and he advocated on the side of women learning.

Jesus not only taught Mary, he taught Martha as well as evidenced in their conversation at the time of her brother Lazarus's death. The Lord revealed himself to Martha as the Resurrection. She answered, "Yea, Lord: I believe," testifying that she understood the remarkable mystery wrapped in the deity of the man standing before her (see John 11:27). Jesus knew Martha was capable of learning and receiving spiritual revelation.

Mary Magdalene

Some theologians have characterized Mary Magdalene as a prostitute, but the Bible tells us only that she had been possessed by seven demons. With such a history she likely suffered from serious mental and emotional issues in addition to her spiritual needs. This desperate woman's encounter with Jesus brought her spiritual deliverance, a renewing of her right mind, and a passion to follow the one who delivered her from her terrible bondage. As a result Mary Magdalene became an ardent disciple of Christ.

The Lord chose this woman to be the first witness to the resurrection. He could have appeared to any number of people who held positions of power and authority—the High Priest, Pontius Pilate, or Peter—but instead he chose Mary Magdalene, a woman whose testimony, ironically, would not have been allowed in a court of law.

It's been said Jesus is perfect theology; in other words, he is the perfect study of God. When we see how he treated women, we know how women should be treated by those professing to be Christians. He talked one-on-one with them. He taught them biblical truths. He revealed himself as Messiah and allowed a woman to anoint him for his burial. He approved a woman's right to listen, learn, and be his disciple.

Following Jesus's sacrifice at Calvary, the veil in the holy place split from top to bottom. Where previously only a representative few had access to the Lord's presence, Jesus opened the way for all. Following the death, burial, and resurrection of Christ, every born-again believer becomes a member of the Lord's royal priesthood (see 1 Pet 2:9). The opportunity to enter his presence is no longer restricted to certain Jewish males, but believing Gentiles—and women, too.

The ripping of the veil at his death symbolized the breaking down of barriers and opening access (see Matt 27:50–51; Heb 10:19–20). Gender barricades were broken. Patriarchal authority (a result of the fall) was no longer the code men and women used to define worship protocols or establish governance in the New Testament church.

A Womanly Issue

In Jesus's day, both Hebrew men and women had bodily discharges considered unclean. An "unclean" status restricted anyone from public contact and by implication from ministry also since a woman's monthly cycle placed her in a position of regularly recurring uncleanness.

One woman who had a twelve-year "issue of blood" pushed beyond societal protocols and touched the hem of Jesus's garment. When she did, the Lord felt virtue leave him. He didn't correct this woman for presuming to contact him in her unclean state, which would by Jewish standards have made him unclean. Instead, Jesus addressed her tenderly and commended her faith. "Daughter, thy faith hath made thee whole; go in peace, and be whole of thy plague" (Mark 5:34). Not only was the woman healed, she gained a new status of "clean" which restored her dignity and reopened connectivity to those around her.

This may seem like a sweet story, and it is. The point in bringing it up, however, is to draw attention to the fact that Jesus purposefully stepped beyond a religious boundary line. In fact, in his treatment of women in general, we never read of any instances in which Jesus treated women as lower in rank or importance than men. One incredible example is found in his remarkable interaction with the Samaritan woman recorded in the fourth chapter of John.

Jesus broke through longstanding prejudicial barriers when he spoke to the woman of Samaria. Jews had no dealings with Samaritans (see John 4:9). Cultural norms combined with racial and religious animosity restrained observant Jews from interacting publicly with most women, let alone one of mixed race and "inferior" religious standing.

Many of the rabbis of Jesus's day would only speak to women who were close relatives. But Jesus came to seek and to save the lost. Although he was fatigued, thirsty, and hungry, he saw something worth reaching for in this broken Samaritan woman and breached several stigmas to reveal himself to her. Not only did he speak directly to the woman, Jesus engaged her in a discussion of theology and doctrine in his longest recorded private conversation.

Jesus often spoke in parables and riddles that forced people to come to their own understandings, but he blatantly told this woman he was the Messiah (see John 4:26). When Jesus's disciples returned from the town they marveled that he had talked with her.

It seems Jesus had preplanned this meeting. Before setting out with his disciples on a journey from Judea to Galilee, he told those traveling with him he *needed* to go through Samaria (see John 4:4). It's a commonly held belief that due to the hatred between Jews and Samaritans, Jews did not normally walk through Samaria but instead purposely travelled around it even when it added length to their trip. While we don't know for certain, Scripture does clarify that upon the group's arrival in Samaria, Jesus sent all those traveling with him away to get food (see John 4:8). It was while they were away Jesus had his conversation with the woman, and when the disciples returned, she went into the city to tell the people the Messiah had come.

Some have said this woman was the first female evangelist. She didn't hold the "office" of an evangelist as commonly thought of today, but the word translated "evangelist" (from the Greek word *euaggelistēs*) means someone who is a "bringer of good tidings, an evangelist."[20] "Glad tidings" is used in reference to the good news or the Gospel of Jesus Christ. Its second meaning is the name given in the New Testament to "those heralds of salvation through Christ who are not apostles."[21] This Samaritan woman heralded the arrival of the Messiah, and many responded (see John 4:39). She was a true evangelist. Her proclamations of Jesus made an eternal difference for those who responded. The result was a two-day revival meeting in her home town—the very community in which she had been an outcast much of her life.

The Lord never restrained the woman from going to the townspeople with the good news. Because of her words many came to faith. From the moment Jesus stepped on the path to Samaria, he knew this woman would "go" and "tell." And he is still calling women today to "go ye therefore."

Dr. Herbert Lockyer, a minister and prolific Christian author of the twentieth century, wrote in his book *All the Women of the Bible,* "With the coming of Christ a new era dawned for womanhood, and wherever he is exalted woman comes into her own."[22] He went on to say, "Through the examples of Jesus in his attitude toward women, and as the result of the truth he taught, women were prominent in the activities of the Early Church."[23] He also concluded that women "came to hold official positions of spiritual influence in the church."[24]

Disciples: Both Male and Female

Scripture identifies the Twelve apostles hand selected by Jesus, but also records many other male and female disciples who traveled with him. A disciple is "a learner" and "one who follows one's teaching."[25] The women who traveled with Jesus were more than curious onlookers, friends, or financiers. They were learners and followers of the Lord.

Jesus broke tradition when he accepted women disciples as part of his entourage. In the past, women had supported rabbis, but the Lord's acceptance of women as part of his inner circle broke contemporary barriers and made a strong countercultural affirmation of women.

Among those who traveled with Jesus, Scripture specifically names Mary of Magdala, Joanna, and Susanna (see Luke 8:1–3). These women were identified as those who "followed him, and ministered unto him" along with "many other women which came up with him unto Jerusalem" (see Mark 15:41). In following Jesus, these women made an *avant-garde* commitment to abandon all, including tradition and accepted social behavior.

Women were witnesses to Jesus's miracles and attendants at his crucifixion and burial. Women were eyewitnesses to the resurrection, and they spoke with the Lord at the gravesite. Jesus charged them with the task of sharing the good news of his resurrection with the men.

The fact that none of the original Twelve were women should be no surprise. Jesus came first to the Jews, and they were living in a time when patriarchy was the rule of the day. Jesus was born into a Jewish-Roman-Greek world that considered women inferior. Even so, many of Jesus's disciples were women. And in the centuries that followed, ministers of the gospel came from all walks of life.

It was always in the heart of God to expand salvation to all the world *from* the Jews, but not limited to them (see John 3:16). In the same way ministry was extended to Gentiles, it was to women as well. The Lord's invitation to discipleship continues to be open to all. What he spoke when he walked the earth is still true today for men and women alike, "If ye continue in my word, then are ye my disciples indeed" (John 8:31).

Joachim Jeremias, a German theologian and professor of New Testament studies, offered this perspective: "Only against the background of that time can we fully appreciate Jesus's attitude to women."[26] That Jesus was revolutionary and courageous enough to accept female disciples is no surprise, but the great courage of the women who dared to break the societal mold to learn from him alongside men should be recognized and honored.

Women Ministering in the Old Testament

Strength and honour are her clothing; and she shall rejoice in time to come.
She openeth her mouth with wisdom; and in her tongue is the law of kindness.
Proverbs 31:25–26

The Old Testament records individuals and groups of women who served the Lord in a variety of roles. One group of women "assembled at the door of the tabernacle of the congregation" (see Exod 38:8; 1 Sam 2:22). The word "assemble" is defined as: "to mass (an army or servants):—assemble, fight, perform, muster, wait upon, war."[27] Author Edith Deen wrote in *All the Women of the Bible* that these women assisted the Levites in preparations for the service. In so doing, they provided "one of the earliest examples of women's ministry in the house of God."[28]

Heman's daughters served in music ministry alongside his fourteen sons. "All these were under the hands of their father for song in the house of the Lord, with cymbals, psalteries, and harps, for the service of the house of God" (see 1 Chron 25:6).

Among the Jews exiled after Nebuchadnezzar's conquest were "two hundred forty and five singing men and singing women" from the tribe of Judah (see Neh 7:67). These likely referred to those who sang in an official capacity. The same word for singers (male and female) is used for those who participated in a religious procession: "The singers went before, the players on instruments followed after; among them were the damsels playing with timbrels" (Ps 68:25).

The Lord chose to speak first to Manoah's wife before speaking to Manoah with the detailed instructions the couple was to follow in raising their son Samson (see Judg 13:2–7). Women greatly impacted their families and communities—sometimes stepping up in unique circumstances. Shallum's daughters worked beside their father to repair the walls of Jerusalem (see Neh 3:12). Moses's wife Zipporah circumcised their children. This was a unique and desperate situation and certainly not a wife's normal function, but Zipporah did perform a priestly duty her husband should have carried out (Exod 4:24–26).

Sarah honored her husband Abraham by calling him "lord" and obeying him, but there is more to the story of their relationship. Scripture records an equal number of times Abraham complied with his wife's instructions as she followed his. God himself instructed Abraham, "In all that Sarah hath said unto thee, hearken unto her voice" (Gen 21:12).

Five Old Testament women are specifically mentioned in prophetic ministry; Huldah, Miriam, Deborah, Noadiah, and Isaiah's wife (see 2 Chron 34:22; Exod 15:20; Judg 4:4; Neh 6:14; Isa 8:3). Women of old were not rebuked for prophesying, but some were corrected when they prophesied their own words (as all false prophets should be). This indicates that women were recognized as operating in the prophetic gifts by the people of God (see Ezek 13:17). Rev. F. W. J. Schroeder noted in the *Commentary on the Holy Scriptures,* "Prophecy in Israel was a gift of the Spirit, and already, as being so, had no restriction as to sex."[29] Not only did he believe this to be true in Old Testament times, he said, "When it [prophecy in Israel] came to be upheld by the Spirit of Christ, in whom there is neither male nor female, this overlooking of all sexual distinctions of necessity still more characterized it."[30]

Miriam, the Prophetess

Miriam. Her name is said by some to mean "bitterness," but one Greek lexicon listed the meaning of her name as "their contumacy."[31] *Contumacy* means "stubborn perverseness or

> **The ministry women performed under the old covenant would not reasonably be restricted by New Testament teaching. No Scripture indicates a cessation of calling and opportunities given to women to prophesy, judge, lead, interpret the Word, lead worship, or announce the good news.**

rebelliousness" or "willful and obstinate resistance or disobedience to authority." Poor Miriam. What a name.

Perhaps a look at this woman through the lens of her childhood will give us some appreciation for the person God made her to be—willful and strong by his design. Miriam, along with her family, was a slave. They lived in Egypt when the pharaoh ordered all male Israelite infants executed at birth (see Exod 1:16). But at her mother's prompting, Miriam intervened and Moses's life was saved (see Exod 2:5–10). At the time of Moses's birth, the babe destined to be Israel's deliverer was in need of a delivering of his own. The situation required a bit of willfulness and stubbornness, and God gave Miriam the strength she needed to stand strong.

Decades later, in the time of Miriam's insubordination, God called her to present herself along with her brothers before the tabernacle. The Lord came down in a pillar of cloud. He spoke specifically to Aaron and Miriam, and God held Miriam personally accountable for her actions (see Num 12:4–5).

After the crossing at the Red Sea, Miriam led the delivered nation in a great celebration (see Exod 15:20–21). The first song recorded in Scripture was sung by this woman. Centuries after Israel's exodus from Egypt, the prophet Micah identified Miriam as one of the three leaders sent by God to rescue his people from captivity (see Mic 6:4).

The Daughters of Zelophehad

In ancient Canaan, five unmarried women presented a legal case to Moses on their own behalf and won. Their father's name was Zelophehad, and he had no sons (see Num 26:33). When it was time for the Israelites to be allotted their portions of the promised land, Zelophehad's husbandless daughters were deemed ineligible to receive their father's inheritance.

With hopes of reconciling their predicament, the courageous women stood before the door of the Tabernacle. There they addressed an assembly that included Moses, Eleazar the priest, the princes of the twelve tribes, and all the congregation of Israel (see Num 27:2). It is remarkable these women were given an opportunity to speak before all Israel on their own behalf. The women successfully pleaded their case and received the inheritance due their father's offspring.

The Jewish Talmud highly honors these women. One translator of rabbinical Scripture said:

It stands to reason that if they had not been ... female expounders [of law], they could not have known the correct interpretation of law, which even Moses, the prime legislator himself, as we see from the context, was not aware of: while we have the Divine testimony to justify the conclusion that they were correct in their exposition, and, in the whole case, a warrant for the inference, which is inevitable, that education in the law was not forbidden to females by Moses.[32]

When Moses went to God for judgment in the case, the Lord said, "The daughters of Zelophehad speak right: thou shalt give them a possession of an inheritance among their father's brethren; and thou shalt cause the inheritance of their father to pass unto them" (see Num 27:7). God did not instruct Moses to correct the women for speaking publicly. Neither did he fault their interpretation of the Law.

The daughters' plea was deemed "right" by the Lord. They received their inheritance, and their courage caused a precedent to be established for women in the future. The Lord said, "And thou shalt speak unto the children of Israel, saying, If a man die, and have no son, then ye shall cause his inheritance to pass unto his daughter" (Num 27:8).

Hannah, Woman of Prayer

A barren woman named Hannah longed to have a child. When she went to the house of God to pray, her inaudible request was so impassioned the priest assumed she was drunk. God, however, understood Hannah's desire. He had compassion on her and opened her womb. She conceived and gave birth to a son she named Samuel, and the boy eventually became a great prophet in Israel.

Hannah brought the child to the house of the Lord to fulfill the vow she made in prayer (see 1 Sam 2:24). As she prepared to leave her son with the priest, she offered a joyful exaltation, and her words became a part of the canon of Scripture (see 1 Sam 2:1–10).

Old Testament scholar Walter Brueggemann suggested Hannah's song paved the way for the major theme of the book of Samuel, the "power and willingness of Yahweh to intrude, intervene, and invert."[33] Hannah's hymn of praise is significant—regarded in Judaism as the prime role model for how to pray—and is traditionally chanted by Jews all over the world on the first day of *Rosh Hashanah,* the Jewish New Year.[34]

Esther, Advocate and Queen

Leadership is defined as influence, and although Esther didn't hold a religious office, she certainly held a position of influence. Her story is the basis for the festival of Purim still celebrated today.

Esther was a Jewish girl who lived in exile in Persia with her cousin Mordecai. Although King Cyrus had given permission for the Jews to return to Jerusalem, Mordecai and his family remained in Persia where Esther was elevated from orphaned exile to royalty.

With no army or armory, God used Esther to save his people. An involuntary hero, Esther pushed past her fears and defied the law of the land by presenting herself without summons to the king. At the risk of death, Esther exhibited courage, wisdom, and integrity. In her time of distress, she turned to prayer and found the confidence she needed to step forward.

Often acknowledged for her beauty, discretion, and good judgment, readers may gloss over the full record of her achievements. The king not only listened to her request, he gave her the authority to determine tactical procedures in a military endeavor (see Esth 9:12–14). Esther played a key diplomatic role that affected the lives of people in 127 provinces from India to Ethiopia. She also regulated how the Jewish nation would commemorate their great victory with an annual feast called Purim. "So Queen Esther, daughter of Abihail, along with Mordecai the Jew, wrote with full authority to confirm this second letter concerning Purim" (Esth 9:29). Mordecai sent letters to all the Jews to establish the days of Purim that he and Esther together decreed (see Esth 9:31). Scripture verifies it was Esther's decree that confirmed the regulations concerning the celebration of Purim (see Esth 9:32).

A nation was saved through the intervention of an orphaned girl, and one of the 66 books of the Bible bears her name. This woman's story of valor and leadership continues to influence people around the world.

Deborah, Judge and Leader

During the time following Joshua's death, the twelve tribes of Israel had no central government. It was the time of judges who served as rulers, military leaders, and legal judges.

Women of Deborah's day didn't typically serve as political leaders, but God used this woman as a judge, a prophetess, and as a spiritual and military leader. Deborah was the third of Israel's judges and she mediated the Word of God to those who came to her. She exercised both judicial and political power. She communicated the will of God to the people and judged disputes in an outdoor courtroom.

For that time, Deborah was Israel's head of state. Her courage and boldness inspired the men to rise in battle against their Canaanite oppressors. Deborah gave Barak, the army general, the opportunity and strategies to lead the charge. He was willing to follow her military orders, but only on the condition she went with the men into battle. Israel's victory over the Canaanites was ultimately credited to two women, Deborah and Jael. Following their military achievement, Israel experienced a forty-year period of peace.

God chose to use Deborah in a culture that strongly favored male leadership. As one of Israel's twelve judges, she may not have established a pattern of women in leadership. She did, however, set a precedent for women to serve in the highest level of Israel's government as a military leader, administrator, and judge.

While she was worthy of many titles, Deborah spoke of herself only as a "mother in Israel" (see Judg 5:7). More than just a wise and bold leader, she had a heart of compassion for the people she served. Also to Deborah's credit, she authored a song of praise that became part of the canon of Scripture. Scholars have called the Song of Deborah the most remarkable example of Hebrew poetry in the Bible, "a specimen of poetical representation that cannot be surpassed."[35]

The Lord entrusted Deborah with the spiritual, civic, and military leadership of his people. She functioned in his plan and with his authority. Deborah was never corrected for being out of order when she served in a position primarily filled by men. Instead, this gracious, successful leader was commended. If God called a Deborah then, he can call a Deborah today.

Jael, Courageous Warrior

Jael, the wife of Heber, was a woman placed in a unique and challenging position. Scripture identifies her husband as a Kenite, a descendant of Moses's father-in-law. Although the Kenites were not Israelites, they lived among the tribes in the southern part of the promised land (see Judg 1:16). Heber, however, moved his family from the rest of his people and set up camp in the north.

Israel's enemy, the Canaanite King Jabin, waged war against them. When Israel's troops won a decisive victory over the Canaanite army, Sisera, the captain of Jabin's army, ran from the battlefield. He sought refuge in Heber's camp, and as he neared Jael's tent, she invited him inside. Given the peace alliance between their people and the prevailing codes of hospitality, Sisera accepted Jael's invitation believing he had entered a safe place.

Exhausted from the battle, Sisera accepted a drink of milk (although he asked for water) and a cover from Jael. He then fell fast asleep on the floor. Jael seized the moment. She picked up a tent stake and hammer. Carefully and quietly, she approached the sleeping man and then drove the stake through both of his temples and into the ground (see Judg 4:21).

In Jael's day women were fully in charge of the tents (and tents could be as large as small houses). They spun goat hair, wove it into fabric, and made their portable homes with their own hands. The women were the ones who set up and took down their dwellings. Given Jael's extensive experience with hammer and stakes, she would have approached sleeping Sisera with confidence she could execute the job—and she did.

Deborah called Jael the most blessed women in the tents (see Judg 5:24). In her song commemorating the victory, she compared Jael with Shamgar, a judge and godly warrior who lived at the same time and who had killed 600 Philistines (see Judg 5:6). The Bible lauds Jael as one among distinguished champions. The *Midrash* (an ancient commentary on Hebrew Scripture) praises Jael among other devout women who converted to faith.

The Kenites had traveled with Israel for generations. Jael would have known the history of the delivering power of God and likely had sympathies for God's people. From her actions it appears she had faith to believe God would deliver his people from their oppressors.

At Jael's hand the captain of Israel's enemy was defeated. It was a bloody, horrific act, but wartime conduct often is. Jael proved herself and her family to be Israel's friends and supporters and secured their future safety.

One Bible commentator said, "This thing was of the Lord, no one can doubt, who considers that Deborah had before pointed out, under the Spirit of prophecy, that the Lord had sold Sisera into the hand of a woman" (Judg 4:9). When Sisera hid in Jael's tent, she used wisdom and the tools she was familiar with to bring him down. She didn't "fight like a man," but she won using her devices, skills, and experiences. Jael stepped outside the bounds of "normal" to perform a courageous act on behalf of the people of God.

Huldah

During the time of King Josiah, a woman named Huldah lived in Jerusalem in "the college" (2 Kgs 22:14). Her husband Shallum was the king's wardrobe keeper and Huldah is presumed by many to have been a scholar who instructed in the college.

Undoubtedly Huldah lived in a place of influence—possibly a religious educational environment. She was renowned as a clear-thinking, godly woman of high social rank, and she enjoyed a good reputation among the priesthood and royal cabinet.

A contemporary of two male prophets, Jeremiah and Zephaniah, Huldah served as a prophetess from 641–609 B.C. During her tenure, King Josiah ascended to the throne at the age of eight. Eighteen years later, a "book of the law of the Lord given by Moses" was discovered during a temple building restoration project (see 2 Chron 34:14). When the book was delivered and read to the king, he instructed Hilkiah the priest and other officials to, "Go ye, enquire of the Lord for me, and for the people, and for all Judah, concerning the words of this book that is found" (2 Kgs 22:13).

Hilkiah and his companions "enquired of the Lord" by consulting Huldah the prophetess. The priest chose this woman over Jeremiah and Zephaniah to interpret the meaning of the Scripture. After hearing the king's inquiry, Huldah delivered a "thus sayeth the Lord"—a prophetic word for the people and their leader. Author William E. Phipps proposed Huldah was the first person ever to declare specific writings were "Holy Scripture."[36]

The priest and officials held Huldah in high regard. Sought out by notable officials, this woman served a significant prophetic role in a pivotal time. By taking the book of the law to Huldah, the fate and future of the nation was placed in a woman's hands.

Huldah delivered the word of the Lord clearly, decisively, and authoritatively. She validated the king's concern that the kingdom was on the precipice of judgment, and the king's response to her words sparked a considerable religious reformation. Immediately after hearing the word of the Lord from this prophetess, Josiah purged the land and reaffirmed Israel's covenant with God. Through Huldah's ministry, revival came to God's people (see 2 Kgs 22:13–20; 2 Chron 34:22–28).

The Old Testament record verifies that many women ministered in various ways in ancient Israel. At times, extenuating circumstances arose and duty called certain women to act in ways that were out of the ordinary. In other examples we see women serving ordinarily in roles such as those who assembled at the door of the congregation or regularly leading in singing. And the record is clear: throughout history, God chose women to serve in specific ministerial roles including prophesying, judging, interpreting Scripture, and leading his people.

Women Ministering in the New Testament

*And on my servants and on my handmaidens I will pour out
in those days of my Spirit; and they shall prophesy.*
Acts 2:18

The roles women served in ministry in the Old Testament were in no way diminished in the New Testament age. In fact, Jesus ushered in a new era for women. From his miraculous birth onward, women played important roles in the life and ministry of Jesus. They were welcomed as his disciples, but some even seem to have risen to the rank of apostle. And after his ascension, they continued their commitment by fulfilling the work of the Great Commission.

Mary, Mother of Jesus and Handmaiden of the Lord

Mary the mother of Jesus has been admired for her devotion and courage. Little is known about her life although some can be deduced from Scripture.

Scripture introduces her as a resident in the city of Nazareth in Galilee (see Luke 1:26–35). Mary was a young virgin—perhaps just twelve or thirteen—betrothed to marry a man named Joseph. The arrival of an angelic visitor frightened her, but her response to his message revealed the depth of her faith. Mary didn't doubt the angel's words. She simply asked, "How could this be?" (see Luke 1:34). Once the angel provided the details her answer was one of a willing, obedient servant. "Behold the handmaid of the Lord; be it unto me according to thy word" (Luke 1:38).

Not long after this encounter, Mary visited her cousin Elizabeth. The song she sang during her visit revealed her knowledge of prophecy. In a time when girls weren't formally trained in the Scriptures, her song affirmed she was well-versed in the Word. In fact, her words became part of the canon of New Testament Scripture (see Luke 1:46-55).

The Lord used Mary as his conduit for salvation (see Genesis 3:16). She had the unique opportunity to be a part of Jesus's life from his conception to his birth, at the times of miracles and teachings, and at his death as well. Scripture identifies her as highly favored and blessed among women.

What did God see when he looked down upon Mary with such favor? She was young, female, and presumably not well-to-do. An unlikely candidate from a human perspective, God saw her heart and a woman of worth. He knew Mary would answer his call no matter the cost. Perhaps it was due to the Word she had hidden in her heart that she so willingly agreed to God's invitation and rejoiced in his plan. She was ready to say yes even to the unexpected.

Mary influenced the life of Jesus. She was the one who urged him to begin his public ministry with the first miracle at the marriage in Cana. Perhaps it was his humanity that led Jesus to respond to her request saying, "Woman, what have I to do with thee? Mine hour is not yet come" (John 2:4). Jesus was in essence saying, "It's not my time yet," but ultimately he deferred to Mary's wishes and turned the water into wine. He submitted to his mother's request and launched his miracle ministry even when it seemingly went against his initial timeframe.

How often Mary traveled with Jesus or heard him speak isn't recorded. She did travel with him and others to Capernaum after the wedding feast (see John 2:12). Scripture bears no record of her personally ministering as a disciple. She did, however, recognize the one she bore was her Lord, God, and Savior (see Luke 1:46-47). She was the first believer in Jesus as the Messiah, and as such perhaps his first disciple. How she must have listened intently to his words.

Mary was the human vessel God used to fulfill Messianic prophecy, and she willingly suffered ridicule to fulfill the purpose of God in her life. Her devotion continued after Jesus's death, and she is specifically named among those in the upper room who received the gift of the Holy Spirit on the day of Pentecost.

Anna, the Prophetess

Anna was a prophetess from the tribe of Asher who loved the things of God. Following the passing of her husband after just seven years of marriage, she spent upwards of sixty years in dedicated service to the Lord. A woman with an incredible passion, dedication, and spiritual hunger, Anna was continually in the temple. She never left. She "worshiped night and day, fasting and praying" (see Luke 2:37).

The Lord honored Anna's singular devotion and sacrifice by allowing her to see the Messiah. She recognized and proclaimed Jesus as Israel's redemption when he was just eight days old.

Anna first saw the infant Jesus in Herod's temple. The massive complex was constructed with four courts built successively. Courts were arranged one behind the other, and a person had to pass through one court to enter the next. Each court was more exclusive than the one before. The first court was the Court of the Gentiles. Next was a divided inner court that had two sections: the Court of Women, where Anna was allowed to worship, and the Court of Israel. The fourth court, the Court of Priests, surrounded the temple building and was only accessible to members of the Levitical priesthood.

It's significant that Anna's declaration of Jesus as the Messiah took place on the temple grounds. This was the Israelite's central place of worship. Anna's public proclamation was made in the hearing of both males and females on the temple grounds, and she continued to speak of Jesus "to all them that looked for redemption in Jerusalem" (see Luke 2:38). This verse indicates that Anna spoke beyond the singular moment she saw the baby Jesus and continued to proclaim the arrival of the Messiah to all who looked for his coming.

When Anna entered the scene that day, Simeon, a priest, was still holding the baby Jesus. Moments before her arrival he made the declaration that he had seen the Lord's salvation and could now die in peace (see Luke 2:28–32). In the Jewish tradition of the day, truths were considered established by the words of two or three righteous witnesses, and the Lord chose Anna to be a witness to Jesus's true identity at his presentation in the temple.

Anna's worship and devotion gained the attention and favor of God and the Lord used her voice to proclaim the arrival of the Savior. She was an eyewitness about whom little is known but so much can be discerned. Her name means "grace" and she was gifted by God to be his prophet and his voice among his people.

Tabitha, the Disciple

In writing the book of Acts, Luke distinguished Tabitha with a unique title of a "certain disciple" (see Acts 9:36). She was a member of the church in Joppa, a seaport town on the Mediterranean coast outside Jerusalem. Her Greek name was Dorcas, but the meaning of both names is "gazelle." The word translated "disciple" in this verse is the Greek word *mathētria,* which is used just once in Scripture. It means "female pupil:—disciple"[37] and is identified as the feminine form of the masculine noun *mathētēs,* which means "a learner, i.e. pupil:—disciple."[38] This language infers that Tabitha was a student and follower of Jesus in the same way men were students and followers.

We don't know if Tabitha served the same functions as other disciples who served in varying roles. It is evident, however, Tabitha was indeed a disciple known and loved for her practical acts of charity. This woman was "full of good works." She continually and diligently worked to serve the poor and widowed in the Joppa community.

Acts of service did not earn a believer a designation of disciple. Works are an outflow of person's faith and followership. Although Scripture is silent about anything beyond Tabitha's acts of kindness, it would be hard to imagine this faithful pupil didn't share the Lord's words with her works—his compassion with her coats and his gospel with her garments.

Told in seven short verses, the record of Tabitha's story began with her death, but ended in a triumphant resurrection. She was so highly regarded that when she died, her church family sent men to fetch Peter from a nearby town. Upon Peter's arrival, he heard the testimonies of the city's widows mourning the loss of their beloved benefactress. He saw the coats the widows held before him while tears streamed down their faces. He sent the mourners away and with godly power and authority said, "Tabitha, arise." The woman sat up and was presented alive to the saints and widows.

When word of Tabitha's resurrection became known, great rejoicing and revival broke out in Joppa. Yes, it was the result of a miracle—a miracle that happened because this anointed disciple made a difference in the lives she touched in Jesus's name.

Philip's Daughters, the Prophesying Ones

In Acts 21:9 Luke established record of Philip's four daughters. Since no wife is mentioned, scholars assume Philip was a widower and that his daughters lived at home with him. The daughters were unmarried virgins, and Scripture says they prophesied. Most scholars believe these were mature women who chose to remain celibate in their devotion to the Lord.

The four women fulfilled important roles in the church. The language of Scripture implies they didn't just prophesy when Paul came to visit, but they were known for being women who prophesied. The Greek literally interprets this way: "But, to this one [Philip], there were four virgin daughters, prophesying-ones."[39] Luke didn't use a noun or a verb to describe the girls, but a present-tense participle that indicated they were prophesying girls. The implication is that the daughters engaged in ongoing prophesying activities.

From the simple phrasing used, it seems these daughters were allowed to freely exercise their gifts of prophecy. Neither Philip nor Paul nor Luke mentioned any objection to the daughters exercising their spiritual gifts.

Although Philip's daughters were unnamed in Scripture, they were well known in their generation and beyond. An annual Greek calendar claims two of the daughters were named Hermione and Eutychis, and that after Philip's death, they went to live with the apostle John in Ephesus. Eusebius, an early Christian writer who lived in the third century, highly regarded Philip's daughters and their ministry. He referred to them as "great lights" in Asia.[40]

The Elect Lady, Local Church Leader

It was a predominant Greek practice to name the recipient of a letter at its beginning. The openings of 2 John and 3 John are identical in structure. The only difference is that in the second epistle, the recipient may have been given a title; and in the third the recipient is clearly identified by name. The latter, Gaius, was John's convert, his "child" in the faith (see 3 John 1:4). Although he was not specifically identified as a pastor, he was clearly a church leader. And it's likely he was the head of a house church overseen by John. The apostle, after all, wrote him concerning the church—in particular, the correct way to handle an issue with a man named Diotrephes. John opened his letter, "The elder unto the wellbeloved Gaius, whom I love in the truth" (3 John 1:1).

In his second epistle, the apostle John opened his letter with a greeting he specifically addressed to a lady and her children. He opened with a greeting to the "elect lady." The fact John was writing to warn her not to allow false teachers into her home indicates she was a prominent woman who likely held authority in the church. The term "house" may well refer to the local church, not simply this woman's familial residence.

Some purport the "elect lady" was another name John used for a local church. However, if the church is the lady, who would her children be? To accept this proposition would mean John was writing his letter to the church (the elect lady) and to the church (her children). This position is weakened also by the lack of any New Testament reference to a local church as a woman or lady elsewhere. The apostle's approach was straightforward. He didn't use metaphors or flowery language in the remainder of his correspondence. There is no reason to believe he deviated from that pattern when he addressed the letter to this particular woman.

Applying normal grammatical usage to *eklektos kyri* (unto the elect lady), the phrase could be translated one of three ways:

- "to an elect lady" (an undetermined person)
- "to Eklekte Kuria" (two proper names)
- "to the lady Eklekte" (a descriptive word and one proper name)[41]

John's elect lady was obviously known and loved by the apostle and the local church assembly he was writing from. "Lady" is the feminine form of the Greek word rendered "Lord," "lord," "master" and "sir." It's a title of honor and refers to "he to whom a person or thing belongs, about which he has power of deciding; master, lord."[42] This is a word associated with royalty, and it is also a proper name. Some translators have rendered *kyria* as the proper name, "Kyria" or "Cyria," a woman's name used in John's day.

Dr. Rendel Harris proposed the identity question of the elect lady was settled "by the discovery in the papyri of numerous instances which prove that kurios and kuria were used by ancient letter-writers as terms of familiar endearment, applicable to brother, sister, son, wife, or intimate friend of either sex."[43] The *International Standard Bible Encyclopedia* concluded, "In the light of this suggestion we should naturally translate, 'to my (dear) lady Eklekte.'"[44]

Whoever she was, the elect lady was a chosen woman of God—one who had authority over at least an estate and who functioned without being under guardianship. Her children belonged to her the same way John's children belonged to him (see 1 John 2:1). The content of John's letter to her makes the most sense when it is read as if he was writing a particular person who served in church leadership.

The tone and pastoral directives John gave indicate his instructions were meant to be applied in the local church not just one woman's family or household.

The last verse of this short epistle is a greeting to the elect lady from her elect sister's children. Taken literally, John was saying the chosen lady had a chosen sister. This sister was also a church leader who had children in the same church John was writing from.

An interesting possibility about the identity of these two ladies comes through the writings of an early church historian named Eusebius. He recorded that in Philip's later years, he and two of his four daughters (the ones identified as prophetesses) lived at Hierapolis in Phrygia. A third daughter lived in Ephesus where John preached. John was the only apostle who lived a long life. Given his close ties to Philip and his daughters, it has been suggested John's letter was written to one of Philip's daughters while she still ministered in Hierapolis. This could be the elect lady, and John may have been extending greetings to her from her sister's church in Ephesus.

In the last part of the second century, Polycrates, the Bishop of Ephesus, wrote, "For in Asia, also, mighty luminaries have fallen asleep, which shall rise again at the last day, at the appearance of our Lord, when he shall come with glory from heaven, and shall gather again all the saints. Philip, one of the twelve apostles who sleeps in Hierapolis, and his two aged virgin daughters. Another of his daughters who lived in the Holy Spirit, rests at Ephesus. Moreover, John, that rested on the bosom of our Lord … also rests at Ephesus."[45] The elect lady and the elect sister could well be two of the "mighty luminaries" Polycrates mentioned or the "great lights" mentioned by Eusebius.

The elect lady of John's affection is one more New Testament example of a woman who served in leadership in the early church and very likely in the position of pastor.

Lydia, Patron and Local Church Leader

The city of Philippi was a prosperous Roman colony, but it didn't have the requisite ten male Jews to form a synagogue. Paul customarily preached first in the synagogue, but in Philippi he found only a group of God-fearing women who met at the river for prayer (see Acts 16:13).

One of the worshippers was Lydia, a successful businesswoman who dealt in the commercial trade of rare purple dye or fabric. She had previously lived in the hub of the purple dye industry in Thyatira and was a woman of means. Purple dye was expensive and highly sought after.

What did it mean that Lydia was a worshipper (also translated "God-fearer")? First, although there were Jewish colonies in Asia Minor, Lydia's ethnic descent is unknown. Her name was not Jewish, but one of foreign origin that literally means "from Lydia," and her home town was located in the ancient Lydian Empire. Lydia may not have been her personal name but instead meant she was "Lydian."

Thyatirans primarily worshipped Apollo, along with Sibyl, Tyrimos, and Artemis. Given the foreign origins of her name and the environment in which she was raised, it's unlikely she was Jewish. However, she could have converted to Judaism. Perhaps through her neighbors, commerce, or staff of servants, Lydia was introduced to the Lord and began to fear him, to seek him. She was a devout woman of faith. Presumably, she went often to the river for prayer. It's evident by her immediate response to Paul how tender her heart was to the things of God.

Since Lydia was the head of her household she was either a wealthy widow or heiress. The lack of mention of either husband or father in a society where women were almost always under legal male guardianship signals her social prominence and presumed singleness.

When Lydia heard Paul speak she believed and heeded his words, and she and the members of her household were baptized. As head of the household she not only led her servants, staff, and possibly family members to the Lord, she took seriously her responsibility to establish them in the faith. This responsibility—along with her personal desire to know more of God—may have been what motivated her to invite Paul to her home.

Immediately after her baptism Lydia extended hospitality to Paul and his traveling companions. She said, "If ye have judged me to be faithful to the Lord, come into my house, and abide there" (see Acts 16:15). This woman had strong communication skills, especially when considering Paul didn't generally accept assistance from new converts. Her offer to "abide" was more than just a proposal that he stay for a night or two. *Abide* means "to remain," "tarry," "not to depart."[46]

Luke, the writer of the passage, said she "constrained" them—a strong word meaning she compelled and obliged them with her earnest, challenging offer. She was insistent and confident, and Paul heeded her request. Her fervor is perhaps better understood when we realize God may well have been answering her prayers when the Spirit led Paul to redirect his travel plans and minister in Macedonia instead of Bithynia (Philippi was a city in Macedonia, see Acts 16:7-12).

Lydia's home became the first meeting place for the church in Philippi, and she became a patron for the evangelists who brought the gospel to her city. There is no record of Paul and his company staying in any other home in Philippi during his first trip or others. Lydia's home could well have become their headquarters in the region. As evidenced by Paul's letter written to the Philippian church years later, her house church grew into a large congregation.

Lydia was Paul's first European convert, and as such the first member of the Philippian church in which she ultimately assumed a position of leadership. Her home could be considered Europe's first church plant. The Bible makes no mention of any person designated by Paul to minister in the fledgling Philippian church. It's likely Lydia continued to oversee this work.

Not only did Lydia and her household host Paul and his ministry team when they first arrived in Philippi, she welcomed them in her home after they had been beaten and imprisoned for preaching the gospel (see Acts 16:40). This was quite a brave move on her part which could have caused damage to her reputation and business. Lydia's leadership may have been more readily accepted in Philippi than in other places in the Roman Empire. The Philippian culture was more favorable to women. Philippi was in Macedonia, and Macedonian women had the benefit of greater autonomy in political, social, and religious affairs.[47] They held significant positions in public life and "built temples, founded cities, engaged mercenaries, commanded armies, held fortresses, and acted on occasion as regents or even co rulers."[48]

In his later writing to the Philippian church, Paul mentioned the women who labored with him "in the gospel" (see Phil 4:3). The record of Lydia's ministry should be particularly uplifting to single and widowed women. Her story provides a strong message that a woman's marital status should not impede her ministry, nor should a woman feel she has to wait until marriage to fulfill her call.

It's interesting that Scripture doesn't document any specific missionary endeavors to Thyatira, but John mentioned a church in that city in Revelation 2:18.

Lydia may have been instrumental in establishing a church in her native community. As mentioned earlier, Thyatira, famous for its dyeing facilities, was a hub in the purple cloth market in which she was engaged. Ancient inscriptions have been found in Thyatiran ruins that confirm the many guilds of cloth dyers in the city, greater than any other city of its day in Asia Minor.[49] With Lydia's commerce and connection to Thyatira via this industry, it is quite possible she played a part or was the direct means in the establishment of a church in Thyatira. Under her godly leadership, Lydia's household of faith grew to become a dynamic and vital constituent of the first century church.

Chloe, Influential Leader

Scripture mentions Chloe just once. Her singular acknowledgement, however, brings several questions to the fore: Who was she? What was her role in Corinth? Just who were the members of "the house of Chloe?"

Chloe is mentioned in Paul's letter to the Corinthian church. The Bible doesn't specify where she lived, but there is no reason to assume she lived outside Corinth. Paul's use of her first name indicates she was well known in the community and that she needed no introduction to those receiving his letter.

It's notable the Greek text doesn't contain any word that would be translated "house" as is rendered "the house of Chloe" in the King James Version. Instead, the language used is *tōn chloēs* which translates literally "those of Chloe." Other translations render this "Chloe's people," "the ones of Chloe," "them that be of Chloe," and "those of Chloe."

From Paul's letter we learn that he was aware of some serious issues in Corinth. He had received a report from *all* of Chloe's people. This would indicate an official correspondence on behalf of the church, not just a report from a disgruntled person or two. Although Scripture doesn't disclose the identity of those who brought forth the report, when Paul responded in writing noting that he had received the information from Chloe's people, he acknowledged the authority behind the report he had received. His writing the letter in itself emphasized the point that the issues at hand were not merely idle tales or complaints. They obviously bore enough weight to receive a lengthy letter of explanation.

Commentators have identified Chloe as:

- A respected member of the church"[50]
- A woman of character and good standing"[51]
- A godly matron and a "good office herein she did her neighbours"[52]
- An "eminent Corinthian lady, known to the Church, who, like Lydia at Philippi, kept an establishment, and her people."[53]

In his *Exposition of the Whole Bible,* John Gill wrote Chloe seemed to be the name of a woman who "very probably lived at Corinth, and was a member of the church there, and at the head of a family of great worth and credit; who being grieved at the growing animosities, and disturbances there raised, wrote to the apostle ... desiring him to use his interest to put a stop to them."[54]

Chloe may well have been the leader of a house church, especially given that no other person is indicated in Scripture as the leader of the Corinthian church. In Corinth, as in Rome and Ephesus, several house churches comprised "the church" of the city. Paul's letter indicates that Chloe contacted Paul because he was the one who had established the work in her area. She had questions on governmental and doctrinal issues and she most likely sent representatives with her written concerns to Paul to get his advice.

Some of the lack of detail about Chloe can be pieced together from issues transmitted in Paul's letter to the Corinthians. Much of the content of 1 Corinthians is Paul's response to the letter he received. He said, "Now concerning the things whereof ye wrote unto me" (1 Cor 7:1). The two primary reasons Paul wrote the Corinthians were to address the divisive spirit and to correct errors and abuses that had sprung up among them.

Whoever Chloe was, she was well known to Paul and the church and was obviously a person of influence. In Paul's day, a letter written to a woman would have mentioned her name alongside her husband or father, but that wasn't the case with Chloe. If a husband or other male had been present (especially one in leadership), he would have been mentioned. Chloe's "people" most likely were the members of a Corinthian house church. If they were simply those of her household, they would still have represented a large number of people. Households in ancient Rome included family, slaves, freedmen and women, aunts, uncles, cousins and even ex-in-laws,[55] all of whom would have been under Chloe's leadership and care. The bulk of the evidence conveys the idea that Chloe was the head of her house and also the leader of a local church that assembled therein to worship.

Priscilla, the Teacher

Political strife uprooted Priscilla and Aquila (a Jewish married couple) from their home when Claudius expelled the Jews from Rome in 49 A.D. Mentioned six times in four books by two different authors, Priscilla and Aquila are always referenced together. In three places Aquila's name is mentioned first, and in the other three, Priscilla is mentioned first. This may not seem relevant in our day, but in Greco-Roman society the man was always named first unless the woman was one of high standing and influence. By mentioning Priscilla's name first on three occasions, at the very least she is considered on equal footing ministry-wise with her husband. They were both valued disciples and Priscilla may have been the prominent partner in ministry.

When Aquila and Priscilla moved from Rome they worked as tent makers in Corinth with Paul. The apostle lived with them for eighteen months before the three left together on a missionary journey. During the considerable amount of time the three lived, worked, and ministered together, there is no indication Paul advised Priscilla to refrain from teaching or speaking in public. If that was his position for all women in all churches, it seems he would have shared it with this prominent ministry couple.

After arriving in Ephesus, Aquila and Priscilla remained in the city while Paul traveled on to Syria. According to Paul both husband and wife were his helpers. They risked their lives for his sake. Paul commended and thanked Aquila and Priscilla and noted their work and sacrifice had such impact it had reached all the Gentile churches.

Priscilla is considered by many scholars to be the first example in Scripture of a Christian woman serving as a preacher or teacher. The couple's ministry to a prominent man named Apollos was significant. Apollos was zealous for the things of the Lord and known for being an eloquent speaker. In 1 Corinthians 4, Apollos was one of the "us" Paul referenced as an apostle in the context of his letter. Paul extensively addressed factions that had arisen in the church in 1 Corinthians. Some people had been divisively contending over which leader they were "from." Some said they were from Paul, others said Apollos, and still others claimed to be from Peter (Cephas).

Why would church members boast about following Apollos instead of a known apostle? The most probable answer is that the Corinthians believed Apollos *was* an apostle, and Paul held this position as well. If he had not, he would have corrected them. Apollo's apostleship is important in the discussion of Priscilla and Aquila's ministry because the two became his teachers in an era when women were forbidden to touch the Torah scrolls or participate in the discussion of Scripture in the synagogue.

> "And a certain Jew named Apollos, born at Alexandria, an eloquent man, and mighty in the scriptures, came to Ephesus. This man was instructed in the way of the Lord; and being fervent in the spirit, he spake and taught diligently the things of the Lord, knowing only the baptism of John. And he began to speak boldly in the synagogue: whom when Aquila and Priscilla had heard, they took him unto them, and expounded unto him the way of God more perfectly" (Acts 18:24-26).

Scripture notes both Priscilla and Aquila invited Apollos, an educated, eloquent man strong in his knowledge of the Word into their home. He was not a child, but a capable teacher and powerful orator of their shared Jewish heritage. Priscilla's teaching of this highly educated man seems to set a precedent. A woman skilled in the Word may teach men—a concept that when applied in our day would include Bible colleges and seminaries.

Priscilla and Aquila's teaching was so effective Apollos was eventually sent by the Ephesian church to Corinth. There he furthered the work in the church Paul, Aquila, and Priscilla had established. Ironically, some of the verses used to restrict women from teaching or preaching were written by Paul to churches where Priscilla was directly involved in ministry. Paul was not shy to call people out who needed correcting; but instead of rectifying a "problem," he praised Priscilla for her ministry and leadership.

Paul called Priscilla and Aquila his *synergos* in Christ. The King James Version renders this Greek word into the English word "helpers," but additional renderings include "a companion in work," "a fellow worker," and a "joint promoter." The word *synergy* is derived from this word which means "working together." The Merriam-Webster dictionary defines *synergy* as "the increased effectiveness that results when two or more people or businesses work together."

Paul was making the point that by his joint labor with Priscilla and Aquila, the work of the kingdom was dynamically impacted with increased effectiveness. He used the word again in reference to Apollos when he wrote that he had planted and Apollos watered, but God had given the increase. These early church leaders were *synergos*—laborers together with Christ (see 1 Cor 8:9).

Priscilla and Aquila hosted a church in their home and likely co-pastored this work (see 1 Cor 16:19). When Paul recognized

> "We can't limit pastoral ministry to a stereotypical gender role; God uses both males and females in spiritual leadership."
> —David K. Bernard, Dth, JD
> General Superintendent,
> United Pentecostal
> Church International

Priscilla as a woman laborer in the gospel, he used the same term he used to describe Clement and Timothy (see Phil 4:3; 1 Thess 3:2). The vocabulary Paul used when noting his co-laborers and colleagues referred to more than hospitality. He considered them his partners in the work of God.

Junia, the Apostle

In his letter to the Romans, Paul praised two particular believers, Andronicus and Junia. These leaders were Paul's blood relatives. They shared his imprisonment for their faith and were identified as "of note among the apostles." In fact, Andronicus and Junia were believers prior to Paul's conversion to Christianity.

In the passages before and after Romans 16:7, Paul listed his greetings to and appreciation of many who served alongside him. What makes this commendation unique and consequential is Junia's gender and connection to apostleship. Of course, Paul recognized the service of many women, but Junia being noted "among the apostles" is compelling—if not pivotal—in understanding the role of women in ministry in the early church.

The first thing to establish before discussing apostleship is the question of Junia's femininity. Most contemporary New Testament scholars agree Junia was a woman. In fact, the majority of Greek New Testament manuscripts refer to her as female. Junia was a popular name for nobility, and throughout early church history Junia's feminine gender was widely accepted.[56] While some have proposed Junia is a Greek variant or nickname for a man, Junia was not Greek, but Latin.[57] Others have suggested Junias (as some later translators rendered the name) is a contraction of a masculine name, but Eldon Epp, author of *Junia: The First Woman Apostle,* found no use of the masculine name Junias in the first century in non-biblical Greek literature and only rare usage in the eras following.[58]

Jerome, a fourth century scholar best known for his translation of the Bible into Latin, referred to Junia as a woman. John Chrysostom, the Archbishop of Constantinople (c. 349 – 407), did as well, which is significant due to his generally negative thoughts towards women. Of Junia, however, he wrote, "Oh! how great is the devotion of this woman, that she should be even counted worthy of the appellation of apostle!"[59] An appellation is a name, title, or designation; and Chrysostom, who was no fan of women in ministry, concurred that the woman Junia was indeed an apostle.

The first to propose Junia may have been a man did so in the early third century. It was suggested by Origen, a philosopher whose views on women in general (like Chrysostom's) were quite negative. Ironically, in his earlier works, Origin spoke of Junia as a female.[60]

According to the *Anchor Bible Dictionary*, "Without exception, the Church Fathers in late antiquity identified Andronicus's partner in Romans 16:7 as a woman, as did minuscule 33 in the 9th century."[61] (Miniscule 33 is an ancient manuscript that included all but one of the books of the New Testament.) The fact there was so little questioning of Junia's gender in her era and in medieval times is remarkable.

Junia's gender has been fiercely debated primarily due to Paul's reference to apostleship. The title "apostle" indicates the highest level of leadership and authority in the first century church. If in fact Junia was a female apostle, her position established a weighty precedent for women in ministry.

The language Paul used—specifically in the English translations of his words— made room for confusion. What exactly does "of note among the apostles" mean? Was the couple just "known to" or "well regarded" by the apostles?

While some have come to the latter conclusion, the Greek indicates Adronicus and Junia were *not* simply "known by" or even "known as" apostles, but were considered exceptional in their calling.[62] Consider the vocabulary and grammar used specifically by Paul, "Salute Andronicus and Junia, my kinsmen, and my fellow-prisoners, who are of note among the apostles, who also were in Christ before me" (Romans 16:7). The word translated "among" is the Greek word *en*. It denotes position and by implication a relation to the rest.[63] This would mean Adronicus and Junia were noted to be "in" the group of people called apostles—"in the interior of some whole."[64]

Looking at the clause "who are of note among the apostles," the two prepositional phrases "of note" and "among the apostles" both modify (are subordinate to and describe) the pronoun "who." The "who" were the "two" (Adronicus and Junia). The two were "of note" and "among the apostles." It would be highly unlikely for the prepositional phrase "among the apostles" to modify the adjective phrase "of note." For example, in the sentence, "The cat is asleep on her bed," both "asleep" and "on her bed" refer back to the cat.

The Greek word *en* is used twice in Romans 16:7. Rev. Kevin M. Shaw explained the language this way, "Just as surely as they were 'in' *[en]* Christ, they were also 'in' *[en]* the apostles." The language indicates that Paul commended Adronicus and Junia as notable fellow laborers and as members of a special group of people called apostles which included the original Twelve, Matthias, Paul, Silvanus, Timotheus, and even Jesus (see Acts 1:25–26, 1 Thes 1:1, 2:6; Heb 3:1).

Paul's usage elsewhere of the word "among" indicates his intended meaning in this passage was their significance within the group of people called apostles. Paul declared Jesus the firstborn "among" the brethren (see Rom 8:29). Jesus was firstborn, and he was one of the brethren. Paul mentioned that he wanted to bear fruit "among" the other believers (see Rom 1:13). He wanted to bear his own fruit, and he wanted the believers to bear their fruit. They were all to be fruit bearers. The angel who spoke to Mary said she was blessed "among women" (see Luke 1:28). Being "among" meant being one of them. These phrases, similar to the one used by Paul regarding Adronicus and Junia, reveal the magnitude of the prestige the ones identified held within the group they were among. In the case of Adronicus and Junia, the apostles.

An apostle is one who is "set apart" and "sent out" as God's messenger to bring the gospel to a place it was not previously known and establish a church. That is what Adronicus and Junia did. They weren't self-appointed, but a God-given gift to the church (see Eph 4:11).

Beyond the debate over her correct title, there is no doubt Junia was a venerated leader in the early church and was honored by Paul as a fellow laborer in the gospel. Whatever "laboring" meant to Paul, he applied also to her as he used the same language when he wrote to the church in Philippi: "And I intreat thee also, true yokefellow, help those women which laboured with me in the gospel, with Clement also, and with other my fellowlabourers, whose names are in the book of life" (Phil 4:3). Paul's fellowlaborerers were engaged in the same type of apostolic work he did—preaching, teaching, and evangelizing. On a side note, tradition identifies Clement (mentioned in the above verse) as the bishop of Rome. Sadly, much of the history of the early believers in Rome was destroyed due to the persecution of Nero and burning of the capitol, but the Bible indicates Adronicus and Junia may have been the ones who laid the foundation for the first century church in the Roman Empire's capitol.

Paul honored this dynamic duo as his relatives, prisoner companions, fellow apostles, and predecessors in the faith. His declaration that they were "before" him may indicate that the two were some of Jesus's earliest disciples.[65] In Paul's acknowledgment of their precedence, he gave respectful and courteous regard to their positions and leadership.

Scot McKnight, biblical scholar and author of *Junia is not Alone,* wrote, "Junia was an apostle. Which means ... she was in essence a Christ-experiencing, Christ-representing, church-establishing, probably miracle-working, missionizing woman who preached the gospel and taught the church."[66] Junia was a person any Christian could look up to as an example of a church leader and an inspiring role model for the called women of God in every generation.

Joanna, Follower of Jesus

Joanna was an upper-class woman in Herod Antipas's court. Married to Herod's household manager, Chuza, Joanna was a woman of high rank and means. Her wealth and position, however, could not buy her health.

At the hand of Jesus, Joanna experienced divine healing from an unknown sickness. Luke mentioned healings that occurred among the women from both "evil spirits" and "infirmities." Whatever Joanna's condition, Jesus cured it.

Joanna became a dedicated disciple and follower of Jesus. She supported the Lord and his disciples in their travels and provided for them financially from her substance. She is mentioned along with Mary Magdalene and Susanna (see Luke 8:1–3). These women traveled with Jesus and his disciples throughout the cities and villages where he preached and shared the glad tidings of the kingdom of God. It was in large part due to the backing of influential women like Joanna that Jesus and his followers were able to travel and minister as they did.

With wholehearted devotion Joanna immersed herself in Jesus's ministry. This woman (who had previously lived a life of opulent comfort) chose to lower herself socially and wander with people of lesser positions as a disciple of Jesus.

Although Scripture doesn't specifically name Joanna as one of the women at the crucifixion, it's likely she was among the unnamed women mentioned who had followed Jesus from Galilee and watched the crucifixion from the distance (see Luke 23:49). These same women went with the men who carried the body of Jesus to the sepulcher (see Luke 23:55).

Scripture documents Joanna's presence at the gravesite on resurrection morning (see Luke 24:10). She held the distinct honor of being one of the first witnesses to the resurrection and even saw the angels present at the tomb. Joanna was privileged to be one of the first to proclaim the magnificent news of the resurrection of Jesus to the world.

Joanna's identity has received speculation in recent years. Some scholars have proposed she is the same woman identified as Junia in Romans 16:7. In Richard

Bauckham's book *Gospel Women: Studies of the Named Women in the Gospels,* he concluded the Roman name Junia (*Iounias*) is a form of the Hebrew name Joanna (*Iōan(n)a*).[67] It's not unusual in Scripture to find people identified by more than one name and in relation to the people being addressed. For instance, the man attributed to writing the book of Mark is called John, Mark, and Marcus. Paul stopped using his Hebrew name Saul when he began his mission to the Gentiles. When multiple languages are used in the same region, multiple names makes more sense.

Dispersed Jews were known to adopt names that fit in with the communities in which they lived. Joanna may have adopted a Latin name close to her Hebrew name. The names Junia and Joanna were both used for aristocracy and were similar in sound. Many indicators could point to the conclusion that Joanna and Junia were two names for the same person. Junia was connected with Rome. Paul stated that she was in Christ before his conversion in 34 A.D. The title "apostle" used for Junia would apply even more confidently if she had been a direct witness of the teachings, miracles, and resurrection of Jesus. Joanna, according to a traditional understanding of apostolic prerequisites (which included being with Jesus from the beginning and a witness to the resurrection), would have qualified as an apostle.

Joanna was part of Jesus's inner circle and is presumed to have continued on with the disciples. Acts 1 notes women in the crowd on the day of Pentecost. Joanna was likely among them, and if so, she would have received the infilling of the spirit of God in the upper room and continued to serve the Lord in his Great Commission (see Acts 1:12–14; Matt 28:19).

Few details are known of Joanna's life but much can be discerned about her character. It is conceivable this woman knew Jesus as well as any—if not most—of his followers. She was faithful to the man and his mission. Scripture records her service to the Lord using the same word for "ministered" (*diakoneō*) as is translated elsewhere in the New Testament for the "office of a deacon" (see Luke 8:3; 1 Tim 3:10). This woman may well have been both missionary and apostle. She was certainly a disciple of Jesus and a blessing to the early church.

Phebe, Deacon and Leader

Who was Phebe? What was her role in the church? Paul's commendation of her in his letter to the Roman church begs these questions and more.

Phebe is perhaps the most controversial woman in Paul's epistles. She received an important letter from him and delivered it at his request to the church in Rome. The apostle documented his approval of Phebe and her standing with him personally and in the church. By calling her "sister" he connected the two of them with the family of God in Rome.

The most interesting word in Romans 16:1 is the one translated "servant." In Greek, Phebe's title is *diakonos*. This word is translated "deacon" and "minister" elsewhere in the New Testament. Given that Paul introduced Phebe as a *diakonos* of a specific church, it's reasonable to believe she held the position of "minister" or "deacon." After all, he was sending her on an official church mission.

Paul commonly made introductions with titles, including his own. He began several letters, "Paul, an apostle" (see 2 Cor 1:1; Gal 1:1; Eph 1:1; Col 1:1). When he introduced himself as a "servant," he used the Greek word, *doulos,* which means a bondservant or slave (see Phil 1:1; Rom 1:1).

Throughout Scripture, when *diakonos* referred to a man, translators rendered the word "deacon" or "minister" (see 1 Cor 3:5; Eph 3:7, 6:21; Col 1:7, 23, 25) but for some reason chose a different word (servant) for Phebe. When Archipus and Onesimus were active or doing *diakonia* and *diakonea* respectively, the Greek words were rendered "ministry" (see Col 4:7, Phlm 13). In fact, the only place Paul used the word with a personal name and it was not translated "minister" was in the case of Phebe (see Rom 16:1). Inconsistent translations, such as in this case, may have influenced the modern understanding of some in regards to the role of women in ministry.

Diakonos in general means "attending to another's interest." In addition to menial duties, *Strong's* outlines its use in reference to "a Christian teacher and pastor (technically, a deacon or deaconess):—deacon, minister, servant."[68] The term is gender inclusive; it's a masculine/feminine noun. Contemporary understanding of the role of deacon often relates it to a specific church office; however, in Scripture it doesn't have a clearly delineated job description. What should be apparent, however, is its gender application.

The same Greek word used to identify Phebe's role in the church appears in different forms throughout the New Testament:

- Jesus said he was a minister (*diaconon*) of the circumcision (see Rom 15:8).
- Paul and Apollos are identified as ministers (*diaconoi*) who caused others to believe (see 1 Cor 3:5).

- Paul and Timothy were able ministers (*diaconous*) of the New Testament (see 2 Cor 3:6).
- Paul said he and Timothy, in everything they did, tried to show they were true ministers (*diaconoi*) of God (see 2 Cor 6:4).

In Edith Deen's comprehensive work on more than 300 women in Scripture, she concluded Phebe "was a Deaconess of the Church at Cenchrea."[69] For those who give little weight to the title "deacon" due to the lack of organizational structure in the early church of an official body of deacons, one important fact should be understood— whatever it meant for men, it meant for women.

In the verse following Phebe's introduction, Paul instructed the church to receive her "in the Lord, as becometh saints, and that ye assist her in whatsoever business she hath need of you: for she hath been a succourer of many, and of myself also" (Rom 16:2). Paul was telling the members of the Roman church that Phebe had been a leader over many and they should make themselves available at Phebe's disposal.

The Greek word *prostatis* is a noun rendered "succourer" in the King James Version. It means "a woman set over others" and "a female guardian, protectress, patroness, caring for the affairs of others and aiding them with her resources."[70] No doubt Phebe held a prominent role in the church community.

First century historian Josephus used the masculine form *prostates* when referring to important leaders and always with positive connotations. Author Aída Besançon Spencer conducted extensive research on the word as used by Josephus in his historical writings. She discovered:

"Moses and Joseph are called *prostates* of the people ... Solomon was made *prostates* of the temple ... Josephus as 'governor' is a *prostates* ... Antipater calls Caesar the *prostates* of the world. God is *prostates* over all ... Clement calls Jesus Christ the *prostates*, the leader who champions his followers."[71]

It seems clear *prostatis* (translated "succourer" in the KJV and "helper" and "sponsor" in other versions) means much more than assisting or providing financial aid. In verb form, it means:

1. to set or place before
   A. to set over
   B. to be over, to superintend, preside over

C. to be a protector or guardian

    i. to give aid

D. to care for, give attention to

    i. profess honest occupations[72]

Phebe obviously held a leadership position in the church in Cenchrea, a port in Corinth. Paul's choice of words lets us know Phebe was a *diakonos*. She served as minister or deacon and *prostatis*, one set in a position of official leadership. The literal meaning of *prostatis*, "one standing before," emphasizes Phebe's position was one of authority, not inferiority.

Paul entrusted Phebe with more than the practical elements of service like those deacons chosen to wait on tables in Acts 6. Surely this godly woman served, but Phebe was also someone who acted with authority. Paul authorized her to deliver his missive to a church he had not yet visited. In it, he spoke of her as a minister worthy to be assisted with anything she required while she acted as his ambassador.

It's highly probable she read the letter to the congregation and answered any questions about its contents. Paul's letter included considerable doctrinal elements that could have been questioned by the people. It would have been Phebe's responsibility to expand on what Paul wrote and clarify any issues.

When Paul identified a person as his co-laborer or fellow servant, he in essence indicated they were in positions of authority similar to his. Some theologians believe women may teach, speak, or preach, but they

> If Paul believed all women were to be silent in all churches, it would have been inconsistent with his position for him to delegate Phebe as his representative and voice to the congregation in Rome.

don't believe any woman should have authority over any man in the church. Phebe gives an explicit example of a woman placed in a position of authority over both men and women.

In the Greek *prostatis* is the noun form of the verb used in relation to deacons. In his letter to the Romans, Paul said Phebe had been *prostatis* over many (see Rom 16:2), and elsewhere he said a deacon was to *proïstēmi* (rule) his own house well (see 1 Tim

3:12). As this pertains to the discussion of women in ministry, we have two possible applications: 1) Phebe ruled over the church, providing for them, making decisions, and maintaining in the same way a deacon should rule over his or her house; or 2) The rule of a deacon was limited to a position of financial support, which seems unlikely and divergent in the translation and Paul's appointment of her as his chosen emissary to the church in Rome.

Phebe was a devout Christian of excellent character, a giver and servant. Theodoret, an influential theologian in the fifth century, noted, "The fame of Phebe was spoken of throughout the world. She was known not only to the Greeks and Romans, but also to the Barbarians."[73]

The women mentioned in this chapter provide ample documentation to the active ministerial and leadership functions women served in the New Testament church. Women were disciples, prophets, and teachers. There is no doubt they held positions of great influence in the early church. The roles and duties women served under the direct supervision of the apostles, they should be allowed to serve in the church today.

Paul and "The Big Three"

Nevertheless neither is the man without the woman,
neither the woman without the man, in the Lord.
1 Corinthians 11:11

For a doctrinal position to be valid it must be based on a true premise that leads to an unalterable conclusion. With that thought in mind, let us make a careful examination of Paul's letters to his son in the faith, Timothy, and the church he founded in Corinth. Much rides on a correct interpretation of a few verses in two letters that have been interpreted by some as restraining women from ministry. I call these passages in 1 Corinthians 11, 1 Corinthians 14, and 1 Timothy 2 "the big three."

1 Corinthians 11

In 1 Corinthians 11 Paul instructed both men and women in the appropriate ways to conduct themselves when speaking in church meetings. He specifically addressed the way Christian women were to present themselves when praying and prophesying. Much attention has been given to defining Paul's teaching on head coverings in this chapter. It's critical, however, when studying, that we don't overlook the key issue at hand. Paul's words affirmed women were indeed permitted to pray and prophesy in public (see 1 Cor 11:5–6). In his letter to the Corinthians he gave women the "how tos" of functioning in these ministry capacities with reverence and propriety. If Paul's intention had been to forbid women from praying and prophesying, it seems he would have crafted this portion of his letter as a correction rather than a teaching on the proper manner in which women were to present and conduct themselves in public ministry.

In Paul's letter to the Corinthians he addressed congregational deeds and functions. Chapter 11 is the beginning of a four-chapter segment in which he specifically wrote on the subjects of prayer and prophecy. In verses four and five, when we read Paul's parallel statements that begin "every man praying or prophesying" and "but every woman that prayeth or prophesieth" respectively, we see Paul was addressing both men and women. Clearly both genders participated in co-ed public prayer and prophecy.[74]

Throughout Scripture women prophesied. Some women believers functioned regularly enough in the prophetic to gain notoriety as women "who did prophesy" (see Acts 21:9). To clarify, the act of prophesying, according to Paul in this letter, includes:

- Comfort (see v 14:3)
- Edification (see v 14:3)
- Evangelistic witness (see vv 14:22, 24)
- Exhortation (see v 14:3)
- Instruction (see v 14:31).

According to the authors of *Why Not Women?*, "'Every woman who prays or prophesies' summarized the full scope of the Jewish concept of priestly ministry. To pray is to speak to God on behalf of God's people or oneself. To prophesy is to speak to God's people on behalf of God."[75] Together, prayer and prophecy demonstrate the essence of congregational worship. Through prayer, those who gather to worship access the presence of God. In response to their prayers, the Lord speaks back through his people by giving prophetic words to those who function in this gift.

In the New Testament the role of priest is no longer designated or functioning in the same manner as it did in Old Testament days. With the death, burial, and resurrection of Jesus accomplished, the role of priest previously assigned exclusively to Levite men was granted to every believer (see 1 Pet 2:9). Men and women speak to God for themselves, receive direct words from him, and intercede for others, as well.

> **In a church comprised of converts from many faiths, the principles Paul taught in 1 Corinthians 11 accommodated the public ministry of women in a society that had previously silenced them.**

While all the specifics Paul was dealing with in Corinth are unknown to us today, we do know the church was a melting pot of people from a wide variety of ethnic groups, social classes, and religions. In each of the cultures present in the church, the hairstyles and veils of men and women held different meanings—from mourning to prostitution.

Gender Distinction ≠ Limited Function

Paul's teaching on head coverings in the first part of 1 Corinthians 11 affirms gender distinction without placing limitations on the exercise of spiritual gifts in the body. In fact, Paul taught that every believer, male and female, should desire spiritual gifts (see 1 Cor 14:1).

Paul clearly recognized a differentiation between women and men, but at the same time stressed their interdependence (see 1 Cor 11:8). He noted:

- Woman came from man
- All men and women enter the world through the womb (mutual dependence)
- Every human is the creation of God made in his image.

In the Creation timeline, Adam was made before Eve; chronology, however doesn't in itself imply superiority or competency. Every man and every woman is the handiwork of God—fearfully and wonderfully made—uniquely gifted and called.

Paul taught men and women how to conduct themselves as they served and participated in the church. His teaching lets us know that a woman's ministry function doesn't override her obligation to appropriately conduct herself in all her life roles. A woman's femininity isn't removed by the infilling of God's Spirit, and neither does a new birth experience disestablish gender distinctions.

Paul explicitly taught that wherever men and women found themselves and in whatever role they functioned, women were women and men were men. When it comes to public worship, gender distinctions should be honored while allowing opportunities for all to serve in the manner established by God for his church, which is a casteless, genderless, spiritual organism.

Headship

"But I would have you know, that the head of every man is Christ; and the head of the woman is the man; and the head of Christ is God" (1 Cor 11:3).

The context surrounding the above verse indicates Paul's audience was a public assembly of believers. His mention of heads in this verse prepares the way for the next two verses in which he spoke directly to both men and women about appropriate conduct in public prayer and worship. The context lets us know the verse is about personal behavior, and not exclusively about "male headship."

The apostle began his teaching in this chapter with the concept of godly order. After praising the church for keeping the ordinances he had taught them (see v 2), he began verse 3, "But I would have you know...." The teachings Paul outlined following these words pertain to what he wanted God's people to know, and that is how men and women should conduct themselves in worship.

A concept of "male headship" or "male authority" as some have interpreted from 1 Corinthians 11:3 has at times been used to limit women in ministry. Let us look to the original texts and see if we can comprehend the true intention of the author.

First, we must recognize the vast horizon of interpretations on the subject of headship. Educated, scholarly, godly men and women strongly support polarizing views. If experts cannot agree, individuals and/or religious organizations may be wise to refrain from using a disputed passage to establish a universal church doctrine—especially when elsewhere in Scripture the same author supports a position differing from a personal interpretation. Since scholars have not reached consensus on the meaning of "head" (the Greek word *kephale*) in 1 Corinthians 11:3, I will not make a dogmatic presentation one way or the other. It's simply not necessary to support the position that women may indeed serve in ministry roles in the church. For your information, however, following is a simplified overview:

Some scholars argue that *kephale* refers to rulership and implies submission. It does in some cases. Other scholars believe *kephale* means "source" or "origin." It does in some cases. In seven places in the New Testament, the word *kephale* was used in reference to Jesus. Christ is the head of all. He is the ruler of all. He is the source of all (see John 1:3–4).

While I do not have enough training in the Greek language to make a case that proves one meaning over the other, Daniel Segraves, Professor of Biblical Theology at Urshan Graduate School of Theology, said, "It seems most consistent to understand the meaning of [head] *kephale* in I Corinthians 11:3 in the same way we understand it in all three uses [in the verse]. If it means something other than source or origin, difficult questions arise: Is Christ not the head of woman as well as man? Must women come to Christ through men? In what sense is God the head of Christ? What are the theological and Christological implications of this?"[76] For now I will leave the debate to the scholars, but consistency and universal applicability do seem to be legitimate factors in making a determination of a word's meaning. And even if a person believes "head" exclusively means "ruler," submission is not mentioned or implied in Paul's teaching in 1 Corinthians 11. In fact, the only authority mentioned is the authority the woman has over her own head.

Context determines how a particular term is being used in a given passage, and the context in 1 Corinthians 11 does not indicate all males have authority over all females. In fact, when Paul said "the head of the woman is the man," the singular use of "the woman" and "the man" indicates he was referring particularly to a husband-wife relationship. With that in mind, it seems Paul was not presenting a creation-based hierarchy in 1 Corinthians 11, but a chronology. "Who came first" does not always indicate "who is in charge." In fact, when we read the Bible, we see many times the Lord chose a younger-born to lead. Moses was Aaron's younger brother (see Exod 7:7), Joseph was Jacob's eleventh-born son (see Gen 37:5–11), and God chose David over his seven older brothers (see 1 Sam 16:1–13).

What lesson then, could Paul have been conveying with his talk of heads? One of the points he made in this chapter is that women, by the grace of God, have their own authority to stand in God's presence (see 1 Cor 11:10). Perhaps the apostle was attempting to teach newly converted patriarchs and pagans the Lord's original paradigm for men and women—one based in Creation itself. Because the first woman came from the first man, she not only reflects the glory of man, she also reflects the glory of God.

SIDENOTE
from Daniel Segraves

The statement "man ... is the image and glory of God; but woman is the glory of man" (1 Corinthians 11:7, NKJV) must not be taken to mean that men are somehow superior to women, for women are also the image of God (Genesis 1:26–27). In this case, the idea is that in addition to being the image and glory of God by virtue of creation, woman is also the glory of man.[77]

—Daniel Segraves, PhD
Author and Professor, Urshan Graduate School of Theology

This is not a place of lesser capability or worth. The woman was created for man's glory, completion, and companionship. Their union blessed both the husband and the wife.

When it comes to the concept of *kephale,* theologians may never come to a consensus of opinion; however, everyone should agree that Paul's message in 1 Corinthians 11 came in the form of a metaphor. He wasn't talking about literal heads, but giving an analogy. This form of speech is especially sensitive to context, and context is critical when making evaluations of Scripture.

Even in the strongest case made for a male, authoritarian, ruling headship, the greatest head of all became servant of all. Jesus served both men and women—unto the point of death. He never attempted to dominate people, and he specifically instructed his followers not to be lords one over another, but to serve one another as he served them. He gave his disciples authority and charged them to minister. Jesus never taught or exhibited male dominance. And in regards to authority in the church, Paul's teachings may well promote quite the opposite of the restrictive interpretations some have taken them to mean.

1 Corinthians 14

It's interesting that while the concept of male authority is often at the fore of the debate on women in ministry, Scripture uses the word authority only once in the New Testament in reference to the relationship between husband and wife. In 1 Corinthians 7:4, before Paul addressed the "keep silence in church" issue later in his letter, he first dealt with the subject of authority in marriage. And he did it in a surprising way. Paul said that a wife doesn't have authority over her own body; but in marriage, she gives that "power" to her husband. He went on to say that in the same way, the husband doesn't have authority over his own body, but yields that authority to his wife. This was a radical statement in a culture where most men considered women to be possessions.

Mutual submission is the very essence of Christ. It's the model and prototype for Jesus's dealing with people and how people, in turn, should submit one to another in the love of God. Serving God is a sweet surrender to him, and it includes giving yourself in service to others as well. This is the polar opposite to harsh authoritarian demands for obedience and submission. The authority exercised by Jesus was firm, but infused with gentleness.

Elsewhere in Paul's letter to the Corinthians, he brought forth another thought-provoking concept. An unbelieving husband can be sanctified through his wife. A Christian wife brings holiness into her marriage even when the spouse is not a believer (see 1 Cor 7:14). Paul asked believing wives to lay down their rights to leave unbelieving husbands (see 1 Cor 7:12–13). These words may be among some of Paul's most unexpected as they indicated a wife had the authority to make such a decision (even if it was not the best decision for her, her family, or the church).

While the message of salvation hasn't changed over the years, methods of worship and church organizations have. Comparing today's structured church services with New Testament house church gatherings must be done carefully and with integrity. We cannot superimpose our modern-day formats upon our perception of early church gatherings. Neither can we assume similarities that aren't supported in Scripture.

For example, in contemporary church services, believers most often sit in seats facing a pulpit on a raised platform, but Paul's writing paints a different picture. In the early church believers predominantly met in homes. People from all walks of life and social classes assembled in environments where everyone was welcomed and encouraged to bring a song or a word similar to Amish and Mennonite practices today (see Col 3:16). In this environment women were free to minister as long as worship was conducted decently and in order.

The problem addressed in Paul's first recorded letter to the Corinthians pertained to disruptions that occurred during public assembly. Apparently some women believers (who should have been listening) had created disorder by asking questions during teaching. A solution was offered to correct this practice that included women holding their questions until they could ask their husbands at home.

It has been proposed that men and women may have sat apart from one another in worship—the women on one side, the men on the other. If this was the case—and women were calling out questions—it would certainly have caused a noisome confusion. Regardless of a congregation's seating arrangement, disrupting an assembly with questions would be out of order and seems to be the issue at hand. Let's look at a passage in Paul's letter that has been the source of much confusion and discussion:

"Let your women keep silence in the churches: for it is not permitted unto them to speak; but they are commanded to be under obedience as also saith the law. And if they will learn any thing, let them ask their husbands at home: for it is a shame for women to speak in the church" (1 Cor 14:34–35).

To correctly apply these verses, we must first understand as much as possible the writer's intention. What message was Paul trying to get across? Who was he writing and why? And then, how should his teachings apply in today's church? What did Paul mean?

Learning in quiet submission was the customary position assumed by novice students. In Paul's day, dialogue was allowed in some forms of education, but not in situations when there were vastly varying degrees of general knowledge. Learning in silence did not degrade an uneducated person. It meant students accepted a position and demeanor in which they learned without challenging their instructor.

Keeping silent and being submitted could have referred to a student-teacher relationship in which disruptive speaking, and not all verbal utterances, should be restrained. For instance, the words "rest in the Lord" reference a silencing of self, submitting to the Lord with an attentive demeanor (see Ps 37:7). Solomon wrote, "The words of wise men are heard in quiet" (Ecc 9:17).

The words in verses 34 and 35 exclusively addressed wives (not all women), which could well indicate the instruction was meant to silence specific women who were questioning and disrupting the flow of service. Verse 35 speaks to the unlearned asking questions in a disruptive manner and doesn't imply barring educated, skilled women from public teaching or speaking.

The case that specific married women were being addressed is strengthened when we consider the remedy put forth to deal with the situation. A woman asking her husband questions at home would not have provided a solution for the comprehensive needs of the church body. Not all women were married. How would asking a husband at home apply to single women or widows? And what about those who had unbelieving husbands, as was obviously the case (see 1 Cor 7:14–15)? Where would women with unsaved husbands receive answers to their questions?

A universal application of silencing all women doesn't seem to be intended. Would a married woman who received a prophetic word first talk privately with her husband at home before sharing what she received from God for the edification of the body? Even if her husband validated her message, when could she share it if she wasn't allowed to speak in the assembly? How would this scenario allow for a woman to be properly used by God to exercise her spiritual gifts? And what opportunity would a single or widowed woman have to share any oral gift of the Spirit?

Paul purposely chose inclusive language when it came to instructing the church on the exercise of spiritual gifts. The word translated "any man" in reference to the one who spoke in a tongue in the church refers to a "certain one" and would apply to males and females (see 1 Cor 14:27). In the verse following the word translated "himself" also means "herself" and "themselves" (see 1 Cor 14:28). Paul's next words were, "Let the prophets speak" (see 1 Cor 14:29). This command had no reference to gender at all, and two verses later he wrote, "Ye may all prophesy one by one" (1 Cor 14:31).

If Paul was truly teaching the silence of all women, he would have been advocating a position that opposed the prophetic word of God that said, "I will pour out my spirit upon all flesh; and your sons and your daughters shall prophesy" (Joel 2:28). Not only that, but a literal interpretation and application of silencing married women would mean they would not be permitted to utter a sound in church. The root of the word silence indicates a verbal hushing—to "command silence by making the sound *st* or *sch*."[78]

Imagine a congregation where women weren't allowed to sing in the choir, pray out loud, teach Sunday school, recite a Bible verse, testify, make an announcement, or even greet a fellow believer. Few churches would literally apply this passage.

> **Perhaps one of the best ways to understand the concepts in this chapter is to determine what they must *not* mean based on other more easily understood passages. Scripture, after all, should interpret Scripture.**

It was Paul's desire that every person in the church would prophesy and speak in tongues (see 1 Cor 4:1, 5). He said that everyone in the church seemed to have something to say—some psalm, doctrine, tongue, revelation or interpretation (see 1 Cor 14:26). And while he encouraged orderly conduct, he never denied the ability of every believer to connect with God and receive something from the Lord to share with the church.

The gifts of the Spirit are available to everyone regardless of gender. Of the nine gifts listed in this same letter many are necessarily oral in nature. Others, to be properly applied, would involve speaking (see 1 Cor 12:8–10), such as:

- A word of wisdom
- A word of knowledge
- Prophecy

- Divers kinds of tongues
- Interpretation of tongues.

In Paul's letter to the Corinthians, the same Greek word is translated "silence" five times (see 1 Cor 14:28, 30, 34). Both men and women were addressed and instructed to keep mute when appropriate for the proper exercise of spiritual gifts. No person or group of people were meant to be silenced for all time. Paul used the word "if" in two of these verses, confirming those silencings were contingent upon certain conditions, not universally applicable to specific church members (see 1 Cor 14:28, 30).

In verse 34, keeping silence has the straight-forward meaning of withholding sound. There is more discussion, however, to be made on the word rendered "speak" in the same verse and verse 35. In Catherine Booth's work, *Female Ministry,* she cited several scholarly comments on this word. She first offered Rev. J. H. Robinson's remark: "The silence imposed here must be explained by the verb to speak (*lalein*) used afterwards."[79]

Booth cited other lexicon listings for *lalein* including Johann Friedrich Schleusner's: "I answer, I return a reason, I give rule or precept, I order, decree;" William Greenfield's: "to prattle—be loquacious as a child; to speak in answer—to answer;" and Liddel and Scott's: "to chatter, babble; of birds, to twitter, chirp; strictly, to make an inarticulate sound, opposed to articulate speech; but also, generally, to talk, say."[80]

Looking at these entries, we can conclude that *lalein* certainly could mean something other than speaking words out loud. If Paul did in fact make a prohibition on speaking for women, it wasn't necessarily a regulation against all speaking, but could apply to improper speaking, questioning, demanding, or babbling. Each of these scenarios would bring chaos into the orderly church service Paul was seeking to promote.

The phrase being "under obedience," according to Robinson, means "to refrain from such questionings, dogmatical assertions, and disputations, as would bring them (the women) into collision with the men." He went on to say, "This kind of speaking, and this alone, as it appears to me, was forbidden."[81]

Considering the ample scholarly definitions of *lalein* and the history of the church before, during, and after these words were written in which women did speak, pray, and prophesy, it seems fitting that godly, educated women be given the opportunity to minister. It's certainly evident it was never the Lord's intention to silence his daughters. They are invited to sing, clap their hands, give words of praise, share their testimonies, and be witnesses for him.

There has been a case made by some scholars Paul was actually quoting Judaizers in verses 34 and 35 and then refuting their words in verse 36. While this is a possibility, it can't be conclusively determined. The words as written and considered in context, however, are enough on their own to surmise Paul would allow qualified, godly women to speak in church.. In reading the apostle's letter with deeper understanding of the culture, grammar, and context, it seems evident Paul wasn't universally silencing women, but was conversely attempting to promote universal, orderly participation in the church body by all. After all, he concluded his discourse with these words (in which "brethren" includes all believers, male and female), "Wherefore, brethren, covet to prophesy, and forbid not to speak with tongues. Let all things be done decently and in order" (1 Cor 14:39–40).

Any understanding of Paul's writings in 1 Corinthians 14 must be kept in context with those in the same chapter in which he used inclusive language when he addressed the whole church coming together and exercising spiritual gifts. Elsewhere in the Word, the apostle spoke positively of women in ministry. Some believe Paul restrained women, but it is more likely he swung doors open for women to minister in their God-given callings.

In the same way healthy families include the voices of both father and mother, God's church will thrive when both women and men speak—in the congregation and in the conference rooms. That said, a woman called to speak should always do so in an orderly, non-disruptive manner—in a way that edifies the body, and doesn't draw attention to herself. One principle should be clear from Paul's teachings. Neither men, nor women, should be disruptive in the assembly of believers.

1 Timothy 2

So much regarding the role of women in ministry rides on the proper understanding of some of the least understood and most contested words in the Bible. Written by Paul to his protégé around 64 AD, 29 words of Scripture's 783,137 words comprise the only passage in the Word of God that explicitly restricts any woman from teaching. "Let the woman learn in silence with all subjection. But I suffer not a woman to teach, nor to usurp authority over the man, but to be in silence" (1 Tim 2:11–12).

A straightforward reading of these verses may seem to present a sound argument against women teaching; however, their same author wrote to, "Study to shew thyself approved unto God, a workman that needeth not to be ashamed, rightly dividing the word of truth" (see 1 Tim 2:15). So let's look beyond the English translation of this passage, beyond twenty-first century linguistics and culture, and to the historical record to see if we can discover what the author was saying, to whom he was saying it, and why.

Verse 11: Learning in Silence with Subjection

"Let the woman learn in silence with all subjection" (1 Tim 2:11).

The word translated "let" is a connecting word. Yes, it begins a new sentence, but it certainly joins the above verse to the verses preceding it: "In like manner also, that women adorn themselves in modest apparel, with shamefacedness and sobriety; not with broided hair, or gold, or pearls, or costly array; But (which becometh women professing godliness) with good works" (1 Tim 2:9–10).

According to these words of Paul, women professing godliness should be modest, given to good works, and must be allowed to learn. He specified, however, they learn in silence. It's important to determine if the apostle was presenting a timeless principle for all Christians in every culture, or if he was addressing a particular situation. To answer the question requires an examination of the historical, cultural, and literary context.

Paul wrote to Timothy with the purpose of giving him instructions on how to lead the church in Ephesus. First Timothy is one of three books considered Pastoral Epistles. The Ephesian community where Timothy ministered was steeped in religious cults, particularly those who worshipped the goddess Artemis. Ephesus was home to the largest pagan temple in Asia Minor. Timothy grew up in this community and undoubtedly understood the pervasive influence Artemis worship exerted in the region. Ephesus was saturated in paganism and close in proximity to Corinth. That is why Paul's writings to the Corinthian and Ephesian churches bear strong similarities.

The church in Ephesus was a composite of converted Jews and pagans. The fledgling congregation was home to some who attempted to blend practices in the worship of Artemis, Judaism, and Christianity. Given the writings of Paul and what is known of Greek society, chastity and modesty were issues among the new converts. Some even promoted heresy. Uneducated, assertive women went from house to house causing problems. There were gossips, and some went so far as to stray from the truth to follow Satan (see 1 Tim 5:15).

The content of 1 Timothy, along with a look ahead into the book of 2 Timothy, reveals a serious problem in the church. People were teaching false doctrine. The Ephesian church had its share of liars who wrongly and brazenly called themselves apostles (see Rev 2:2). Paul also noted there were those who desired to be teachers of the law but didn't understand it (see 1 Tim 1:7).

As touched on in the previous section, in the era Paul penned his words, learning in silence was not an insult but an uplifting to women who had previously been banned from the opportunity for religious education. Aida Besançon Spencer, in her book *Beyond the Curse,* concluded that silence was a "positive attribute for rabbinic students. Paul's words declared to his Jewish friends that women should be learning the same way rabbinic students learned."[82]

Simeon, the son of Rabbi Gamaliel (Paul's famous teacher who was a leading authority in the ancient Jewish court in the early first century) said, "All my days have I grown up among the Sages and I have found naught better for a man than silence."[83] Not only were learners to be silent, but silence was venerated and practiced by both learners and the wise. From this viewpoint, it could be considered that Paul was treating women as having the potential and opportunity to be wise students.

The word Paul used for "learn" is the Greek word *manthanō,* which means:

>to learn, be appraised
>
>1a) to increase one's knowledge, to be increased in knowledge
>
>1b) to hear, be informed
>
>1c) to learn by use and practice
>
>1c1) to be in the habit of, accustomed to[84]

Manthanō was written in present tense, which means it was a statement of fact or reality at the time it was written. The mood of the word is imperative, which means it "expresses a command to the hearer to perform a certain action by the order and authority of the one commanding."[85] Paul was in essence saying, "Learn now, ma'am. Get into the habit of increasing your knowledge and being informed." His use of the word *manthanō* was significant because it implied formal religious training. It was the word used by the Jews who were astonished at Jesus's teaching. They asked, "How is it this Man has learning [is so versed in the sacred Scriptures and in theology] when He has never studied?" (John 7:15, AMPC).

Paul was expressing a positive opportunity for women to learn. Learning in silence and submission, according to author David Hamilton, "was a frequent formula in the Near East for a model student."[86] It indicated having a teachable attitude—the attitude expressed in James 1:19, "Let every man be swift to hear, slow to speak, slow to wrath." Paul was saying to these women who had never been allowed scholarly education in the synagogue—if they approached learning with an attitude of humble submission, they could have access to the same education male disciples enjoyed. Spencer's research agreed with Hamilton's: "Ancient Jews esteemed silence as a state of calm, restraint at the proper time, respect and affirmation of a speaker."[87]

The word translated "silence" in this passage is not the same as the shushing in 1 Corinthians.[88] It doesn't mean silence as in muzzling, being speechless, being still, or even holding your peace. It has to do with quietness. In fact, the same word was used when Paul addressed the Jews, "And when they heard that he spake in the Hebrew tongue to them, they kept the more silence" (Acts 22:2). In this situation, the people who had been in an uproar chose to still themselves to give Paul their full attention. Quietness connotes deference; it's a respectful submission as opposed to resisting, striving, or arguing.

The root of the word translated *quietness* was used earlier in this same chapter when Paul spoke of living a "peaceable life in all godliness and honesty" (see 1 Tim 2:2). Certainly Paul didn't mean people should live without speaking. Peter also spoke of having a "meek and quiet spirit, which is in the sight of God of great price" (see 1 Pet 3:4).

Learning with a still spirit is the right way for a serious student to learn the ways of the Lord and should be a desire of every believer, male and female. Paul's words, rather than being a derogatory regulation, offered respect to a woman's ability to learn. The true import of his statement was that the woman should no longer be restricted from learning. He quite adamantly told the church she *should* learn—she *must* learn. What some consider harsh words went a step beyond a gracious invitation and made a strong statement to the men, "Let her learn." In the patriarchal culture of Paul's day, the apostle believed and taught women should be granted an education where it had been previously withheld. In fact, educating the uneducated would be his remedy for false teaching in the church.

Verse 11 of 1 Timothy 2 specified that women were to learn "with all subjection." The word translated "subjection" is the same Greek word Paul used when he spoke to both men and women who were obediently subjecting themselves to give to the church (see 2 Cor 9:12–13). All believers, male and female, are to be in subjection to the Word of God.

The Woman in Ephesus

It's important to note how Paul transitioned from speaking from the manner in which men and women should conduct themselves (verses 8–9) to address "the woman" (verse 12). He switched from plural to singular, and then back to plural. This could certainly indicate his restriction was meant for one specific Ephesian woman. In that case, "the woman" who had caused damage in the church (likely by teaching false doctrine) was to be silenced and instructed in the truth. Regardless of gender, any person displaying this conduct should be corrected. If this was Paul's motive, his words demonstrated a pastoral heart that exercised patience and loving discipline.

If Paul had indeed restricted a singular woman from teaching in answer to a specific issue in the Ephesian church, it is simply reading too much into the text to suggest he was establishing a universal church policy for all time and all people. If that was his intention, there should be evidence in Paul's other writings or other places in the Word of God. Remember, for a doctrinal position to be valid it must be based on a true premise that leads to an unalterable conclusion. Since the information on Paul's writings in 1 Timothy is incomplete (a one-sided conversation), probability comes into play. In other words, given what is known, what is the most likely scenario?

In 1 Timothy it's evident there was a serious situation with false teaching in the church. Paul opened his letter with a request that Timothy stay in Ephesus because false doctrine was being taught (see 1 Tim 1:1–3). Within the chapter are further references (see 1 Tim 1:10, 19, 4:1–3), and the letter concluded with Paul's charge to Timothy to keep what had been entrusted to him and not get entangled with some who professed faith but erred concerning it (see 1 Tim 6:20–21).

Paul's concern for the false teaching in Ephesus is part of a theme that runs throughout his letter. In his correspondence he also mentioned some women who were wandering from house to house, "tattlers also and busybodies, speaking things which they ought not" (see 1 Tim 5:13). Not all women were doing this, but some were, and the specific situation needed to be addressed.

It stands to reason that in 1 Timothy Paul instructed the young minister to silence false teachers. This doesn't of necessity apply to godly, educated women. In fact, later Paul reminded Timothy of the spiritual heritage he had received from his mother and grandmother (see 2 Tim 1:15). Paul didn't correct Timothy for listening to women. Instead, he commended the women who had passed on a true, pure faith in God. That was a beautiful heritage.

Verse 12: Teaching and/or Usurping

In verse 12 Paul continued his instructions with these words: "But I suffer not a woman to teach, nor to usurp authority over the man, but to be in silence." In contemporary vocabulary, the word *suffer* has a negative meaning, but Jesus used it to express his positive desire to allow children to come to him. He said, "Suffer little children, and forbid them not, to come unto me" (Matt 19:14).

The verb in this sentence (suffer) is present tense. In other words, the verse could accurately be translated, "I am presently not permitting or allowing a woman to teach." The use of this tense implies a temporary policy. Why would Paul state these words about teaching right after instructing the woman to learn? A logical answer would be that in order to teach, one must first learn, and the woman was just beginning to receive instruction.

When a person meets necessary moral and educational qualifications, any previous prohibition to teach could be lifted. This harmonizes with the whole of Scripture, for if Paul truly restricted women from speaking everywhere, how could he reconcile that position with biblical precedents? Women like Miriam, Deborah, Priscilla, and Huldah spoke, prophesied, judged, and taught. It would have been a notable contradiction, and the Word of God does not contradict itself.

Paul was a master wordsmith who chose his words carefully. His temporary injunction "not allowing a woman to teach" was in stark contrast to the strong command that came directly before it, "Let her learn." One of Paul's contemporaries was Philo of Alexander. He was a Hellenistic Jew thoroughly educated in Greek philosophy and culture. Philo said, "Ignorance is an involuntary state, a light matter, and its treatment through teaching is not hopeless."[89] There is a cure for lack of education: education.

Teaching, however, must be done by one who is competent. The Greek word *didaskō* translated "teach" in this passage means "to hold discourse with others in order to instruct them" and "deliver didactic discourses." Didactic teaching is formal, lecture-style teaching usually intended to give moral instruction. If the woman in Ephesus was not learned, she was not ready to teach.

Teaching conducted in the first century church was different from what we see in today's pulpit ministry. The teaching taking place in the early church was primarily transmitting the gospel: the death, burial, and resurrection of Jesus. It included teaching on spiritual growth and how to live as a church body, but it was not likely exegetical biblical instruction of Old Testament Scripture (exegetical meaning critically explained or interpreted). It was certainly not expository teaching that detailed the meaning of New Testament writings because at that point, what is now New Testament canon was in the form of letters circulating from church to church. The Bible had not yet been assembled.

It seems reasonable Paul's goal was to ensure qualified teachers instructed those who came together for worship. He wrote elsewhere, "And the things that thou hast heard of me among many witnesses, the same commit thou to faithful men, who shall be able to teach others also" (2 Tim 2:22). The word translated "men" in this verse is the Greek word *anthrōpos,* which means "a human being, whether male or female." If it had been Paul's intention to restrict all women from teaching, he could have chosen a gender-specific word. Instead he deliberately, under the inspiration of God, chose a word that represented all humanity.

In the Greek, verses 11 and 12 are one sentence. The transition word of verse 12 translated "but" is *de* in the Greek. It is an adversative particle which means it expresses opposition. It is "used to connect one clause with another when it is felt that there is some contrast between them, though the contrast is often scarcely discernible."[90] Paul was in effect saying, "Let the woman learn, but (in contrast, however) I am not allowing her to teach. The *de* was placed between the two thoughts because there is some contradiction, some tension between them. Why would a woman learn and not be able to share what she has learned with others?

Some would cite 1 Timothy 2:11–12 as a proof text that women should not hold teaching positions or otherwise minister in the church. These two verses, however, should not be isolated from their biblical context. Paul sandwiched his "not teaching" instruction between two "learn" statements. In a church full of new converts—some coming from a very different world than an ordered, respectful church environment—Paul required the young Christians to be restrained learners, not to assert themselves, but to receive instruction. In other words, a learner must earn their credentials before attempting to teach.

It should also be considered in this personal letter written by Paul to Timothy that although the apostle conveyed his advice and the reasoning behind his words, he didn't say, "thus saith the Lord." He didn't use strong words like "ought" and "duty" and "must needs" and "bound" as he did in other portions of Scripture (see Rom 15:1, 27; 1 Cor 11:7, 10; Eph 5:28). Paul's advice to Timothy to handle this particular church situation should not be treated as a mandate for all churches at all times.

Authority

"But I suffer not a woman to teach, nor to usurp authority over the man, but to be in silence" (1 Tim 2:12). I've often wondered why Paul, who was such a wordsmith and scholar, chose to use the word *authenteō* (translated "authority" in verse 12) only once in all his correspondence and teaching. Think about it. Able to communicate in Greek, Hebrew, Aramaic, and likely Latin, he dropped this word in the middle of what would become one of the most controversial passages in the Word of God. *Authenteō* was not the word he used dozens of other times for exercising authority. If Paul had meant the conventional operation of authority, he had several other words to choose from. Many problems could have been avoided if he had simply selected another word that had a more widely understood definition. But he chose it on purpose. Paul used uncommon vocabulary for an uncommon situation.

Authenteō is a rarely used word that has a violent association. "In the earlier usage of the word it signified one who with his own hand killed either others or himself. Later it came to denote one who acts on his own 'authority;' hence, 'to exercise authority, dominion.'"[91] This word was associated with extreme abuse of power and exercising absolute mastery over others. Josephus (a first century Roman-Jewish historian) used the noun form of the word to render the word "assassins."[92]

Since the word *authenteō* is used only once in Scripture, any meaning found for it must be limited to fit within the constraints of the subject at hand. In extra-biblical writings, the word is infrequently used, which makes it difficult even for experts to come to a consensus as to its meaning at the time of Paul's writing. In the case of 1 Timothy, the word is in the middle of Paul's teaching on the outward behavior of church members especially relating to appropriate dress, manner, and conduct.

Authentein is joined to the word translated "teach" by the word *oude. Oude* is a conjunction that requires the person writing to keep the same perspective on what comes before and after. If either the "teaching" or "authority" can be proven to be positive or negative, the other connected word will have the same meaning.[93] The implication is that since Paul used *authenteō* in the context of Christian conduct and keeping uneducated or misinformed women from teaching, the word relates to the women's deportment. This would refer to conduct, behavior, attitude, and even facial appearance. Noel Bullock, who wrote on the subject for a theological journal, said, "Literary context suggests that something about their demeanor seemed forceful or heavy-handed."[94] It seems a domineering demeanor is the issue, not having authority, which in itself can be neutral, positive, or abused. Additionally on the subject of *oude,* some scholars believe the word would be more appropriately translated "in a manner of," which would render Paul's prohibition "teaching in a manner of usurping." Usurping means to seize and hold a position by force or without legal right.

It is possible *didaskō* (teaching) and *authenteō* (usurping authority) were purposely paired together to make a singular point. Paul utilized this writing technique elsewhere in the same letter. For example, he paired words like prayers and petitions, peaceful and quiet, godliness and holiness, good and acceptable. Coupling *authenteō* and *didaskō* could indicate that both words apply to the same activity: forbidding women to teach heresy to men with a domineering approach and bearing.

Philip Barton Payne, a specialist in New Testament studies agreed. He said, "In the Pauline corpus, *oude* is usually employed to bring together two closely related ideas."[95] He further clarified the words teaching and authority connected by *oude* indicate "*authentein* explains what sort, or what manner, of teaching is prohibited to women."[96] He offered this example: "If we should say, I forbid a woman to teach to discuss differential calculus with man, it becomes clear that the subject in which she could not give instruction is high mathematics."[97] In this case, Paul would not have allowed a woman to teach men in an overbearing, tyrannical manner.

Regardless of gender, it's never right for a teacher to domineer. That was not Paul's approach, nor was it the manner Jesus used to convey his message. The bottom line is this: no one is to assume authority for their own purposes—to wrest it for themselves instead of receiving it from God with confirmation from their spiritual leadership. Peter concurred with this concept when he told the elders to refrain from dictatorially leading the flock (see 1 Pet 5:3). Nadab and Abihu provide a sobering example of what happens to those who operate under their own authority (see Lev 10:1–2).

With so much uncertainty surrounding 1 Timothy, two things are evident: it is unclear and uncertain. To appeal to this passage as the cornerstone for doctrines and practices for women in ministry is problematic at best. A vaguely understood passage should be held against the light of those more easily comprehended. In context, it appears Paul was explaining to Timothy that women were not to usurp, hijack, or commandeer authority God did not give them. It's not hard to imagine some of the women who had been raised in the pagan culture or converted from restrictive Judaism were anxious to be involved. Perhaps even with good intentions, some overstepped; and perhaps that is why Paul's response, when properly understood, was so gracious.

Paul wanted to make sure Timothy knew his duty to ensure teachers were doctrinally sound. Any person teaching false doctrine should not be given a forum in the church. Any ministry must be conducted under proper spiritual authority, and any teacher who would pervert the Word of God should not be given a position of influence.

While some (who truly believe they have sound biblical backing) would silence all women from teaching or even speaking, the issue at hand applies equally to both genders. In the same way a man could err by teaching while usurping authority, conversely a woman could teach and *not* usurp authority. A woman can teach without an arrogant, bossy manner of presentation—and without presuming absolute mastery over others.

The concept in question is a person seizing what does not belong to him or her—of acting for oneself. If a woman is under her spiritual authority, especially if she has received a license from her church organization, she is not usurping, she is serving. She is not domineering; she is doing the work of the Lord according to his call on her life.

A proper application of Paul's intention in this verse puts to rest the misunderstanding that he was forbidding all women from holding positions of authority. One thing is certain: *authenteō* is not *exousia*, the word used for exercising authority. Paul used a far different word that represented vulgar abuse of authority. He didn't forbid women from possessing and utilizing *exousia*. Perhaps Paul did, after all, do what was best when he penned that little-known word to make a strong differentiation between the type of authority he was addressing.

The apostle Paul didn't close doors for women. He invited them to participate in a new era. Now they may learn. They must learn. But as beginners, they must conduct themselves calmly and exercise restraint in the educational process as they receive and assimilate sound doctrine. Paul's teaching in the first century church is applicable to the church today. The uneducated must first be trained before they speak. If they are engaged in false teaching, they must be silenced and instructed. If their motive is for self or domination, they must be restrained and lovingly disciplined.

> **Note that in the King James Version the translators specifically rendered *authenteō* in a way that doesn't bar a woman from having authority, but forbids her usurping authority.**

Oftentimes the controversy involving women in ministry is rooted in the subject of who holds authority. Sadly, there are those who misunderstand the Word and consider any position of authority to automatically belong to men. At the time Paul authored his letter to Timothy, the New Testament was neither complete nor considered sacred. Authority was God-given then, as it is today. Since the completion of the full canon of Scripture, believers turn to the Word of God as the source and validation for all authority.

Should a woman have authority over a man? In truth, every believer is a volunteer in the kingdom of God, and every individual chooses to submit him or herself to God and his Word. True authority rests on the Word. No preacher or teacher can force anyone to do anything he or she doesn't choose to do. Any teacher, preacher, or person in a position of authority who operates outside the parameters of the Word wields power but no true authority. But when a woman ministers under the covering and blessing of her spiritual authority and in agreement with the call of God on her life, any authority she exercises is based on the Word, not the woman. The proper motive for ministry is working to fulfill the Great Commission, not to gain authority or position.

The call to pulpit ministry may never be proportional between men and women, and it may not always be as comfortable for women in certain settings, but it's okay for people to be in the minority when they are in the will of God. What is comfortable or familiar is not necessarily what is right and best. That applies to organizational leadership and members of the congregation as well. Being in God's will is more important than staying in the comfort of the familiar.

When we look to the Bible we see the church is not the originator of authority, but is the recipient of authority delegated from the Lord for the oversight and care of his people. Spiritual authority isn't something to be gained by self-promotion or demanding "rights" to minister. Samuel Brengle, an early commissioner in the Salvation Army, expressed it this way, "It (spiritual authority and leadership) is attained by confession of sin, and much heart-searching and humbling before God; by self-surrender, a courageous sacrifice of every idol, a bold uncomplaining embrace of the cross, and by an eternal, unfaltering looking unto Jesus crucified."[98]

Authority in the New Testament Church

New Testament writings affirm a collective authority in the church. There is not one chief, absolute position of authority among God's people. In Bible days, spiritual and doctrinal authority rested not with a local pastor, but collectively. The biblical precedent was one of interchurch accountability, control, and management. When a question arose about what should be required of Gentile converts, a council met, came to a consensus, and then issued a protocol they expected to be implemented in all the local churches (see Acts 15:2–35). When Peter stepped outside the conventional parameters of Judaism to preach to the Gentiles, he was held accountable by the church (see Acts 11:2, 18). Paul, who taught and trained others, submitted to the directive of the church when he and his traveling companions arrived in Jerusalem (see Acts 21:17–26).

When the apostles died, one by one, God-called and commissioned believers continued the work that endures today. We never see biblical record of dictatorial power or controlling leadership in the early church. Dominating and controlling others with any type of compulsion or intimidation is rebellious and dangerous for all those involved.

Biblical authority flows from God's chosen vessels. In the Garden, God gave rulership to both Adam and Eve. He created them excellent in every way and gave them dominion over all the earth to bless it and protect it. Authority can flow from a man or a woman, but its origin is God, and it is meant to be used to influence others for good. Any authority given to God's people is given to serve under one supreme ruler, and that is the Lord Jesus Christ (see Matt 28:18). He is the one who chooses and commissions disciples to preach the gospel message.

For those who profess a literal application of the English translation of 1 Timothy 2:11–12, a faithful interpretation of Scripture would mean all Paul's instructions should be followed in the same way they were written in the epistles. In 1 Timothy 5, for instance, Paul gave lengthy regulations about the care of widows. In chapter 6 he gave instructions to slaves and masters. According to Paul's other writings (four times in the New Testament), all Christians should greet one another with a holy kiss.

To be consistent, if 1 Timothy 2:11–12 teaches a universal truth, no Christian female with integrity should teach males in Sunday school, public school, or homeschool. On the other hand, however, if it is biblical and appropriate for a woman to teach in Sunday school or on a mission field, it's only logical she should be allowed to speak elsewhere, including a church pulpit.

If in his letter Paul was reemphasizing an established tenant of the faith to Timothy—that women should be silent—of the thirteen to fourteen letters Paul authored, we would expect to find reiterations of this "truth." Given the huge implications these instructions would have on every church, it stands to reason Paul would have mentioned them to the churches he wrote in nine other locations, especially in the epistles in which he dealt with the roles and function of ministers in the churches. Would he not have at least advised Timothy to circulate this letter to other churches? And why did other key apostles like Peter and James neglect to support or transmit this concept in their writings?

Paul commended Priscilla, a teacher and founding leader in the Ephesian church Timothy oversaw. The present tense of Paul's prohibition in verse 12 indicates he would not apply a teaching restriction to women like Priscilla who taught truth (see Acts 18:26). If women-led ministry was contrary to Paul's understanding of God's will, he would not have praised Priscilla as his helper in Christ, but corrected her erroneous ways.

In two other books considered Pastoral Epistles, Paul directly addressed false teaching problems and how they were to be handled (see 2 Tim 2:16, 25–26; 3:5; Titus 1:10–11; 3:10–11). Linda Belleville wrote in *Women Leaders and the Church* that

35 percent of the content of Paul's first letter to Timothy dealt with correcting false teaching.[99] Among the false teachers were women and men, including two men named Hymenaeus and Alexander (1 Tim 1:20). That Paul was dealing with a specific situation in Ephesus is reemphasized by his warning that wolves had entered the church to hurt and hinder (see Acts 20:29). This is what happens when people teach doctrine contrary to the established teachings of the church.

The backdrop for 1 Timothy 2:8–15 is false teaching. It is against this backdrop Paul's words unfold, progress, and build. This unit of Scripture should not be interpreted apart from its context in this chapter or in the whole of the Word. Its language is tied to the rest of Paul's letter. Understanding his intent is the key to unlocking this passage that is a portion of Paul's appeal for appropriate behavior of both men and women in their homes, in the church, and in their community.

The context is public prayer, specifically prayer everywhere, not just in an assembly of believers. In verse 8 Paul expressed his desire that men should pray everywhere with uplifted, holy hands, without wrath and doubting. The next verse begins "in like manner also." Paul linked the instruction on prayer given to men with instruction on prayer to women. He said women should present themselves modestly when they pray. Paul made a presupposition (similar to what he stated in 1 Corinthians 11) that women would pray in public. Women were not silenced, but instructed in the correct conduct as they spoke.

Sir William Ramsay, a Scottish archaeologist, New Testament scholar, and professor, believed the use of "likewise" connected verse 9 with the subject in the previous verses, which is prayer. Ramsay wrote, "The necessary and inevitable sense of the word ["likewise"] is that the whole body of women is to be understood as affected by what has been said about men."[100] He believed the sentence was wrongly punctuated and that Paul wanted women to pray everywhere—just as he had expressed this desire to the men. With the current punctuation, a literal interpretation of the Scripture would render a non-biblical position: that women should dress in the same manner as men who were to be praying with uplifted hands.

The Husband and the Wife

What exactly does it mean that "a woman" is not allowed to teach or usurp authority over "the man?" The Greek word interpreted "woman" most often means "wife." The Greek word translated "man" refers to either a husband or a betrothed or future husband. Note that *woman* and *man* are both singular in this verse. If these words referenced a husband and wife, Paul's instruction meant that a wife should not take authority over her husband. In this case, the issue had nothing to do with every woman being subject to every man.

Today, wives who would never dream of stepping into a pulpit but regularly boss their husbands around are the ones who are most likely disobeying Paul's teaching. A wife was to learn, but not instruct (tell what to do) or dominate (have authority over) her husband. In conversation, Rev. Kevin M. Shaw offered this thought, "The apostle Paul was pretty 'dead-set' against bossy wives. Sadly, people who think 1 Timothy 2:11–12 is about preaching or pastoring actually miss the full impact of what Paul is teaching."

We would be hard pressed to find evidence 1 Timothy 2:11–12 refers to the public function or ministry of women in the church as it is often applied. Many scholars believe these verses were written about the relationship between a husband and wife in their home. Rev. J. H. Robinson wrote in regards to this passage, "It is primarily an injunction respecting her personal behavior at home. It stands in connection with precepts respecting her apparel and her domestic position; especially her relation to her husband."[101]

Robinson went on to say in this same work, "The 'teaching,' therefore which is forbidden by the apostle, is not every kind of teaching ... but it is such teaching as is domineering, and as involves the usurpation of authority over the man. This is the only teaching forbidden by St. Paul in the passage under consideration."[102]

The type of teaching being forbidden in the passage is dictatorial and domineering—a taking "absolute mastery" over another. Given this information, an alternate (paraphrased) version could be rendered, "I do not allow a wife to teach absolute mastery or commandeer God's authority over her husband. Instead, she should learn in agreement with Scripture, giving deference and respectful submission to its authority and the authority God has placed in her life."

A strong case can be made that Paul's words addressed the conduct and character of a wife with her husband. In this case, the instruction would not apply to women in right biblical relationship with their spouses and would lead to the conclusion the passage does not effect a woman's call to preach or teach.

Apostle Paul, Friend and Advocate

Paul understood deep things in God, but many have misunderstood him. Paul insisted true worshippers were not saved by following the jots and tittles of the old rabbinical law. Ironically, over time church leaders developed "Pauline theology" that suggests this champion of grace became the New Testament church's primary lawgiver.

Lack of understanding by people in contemporary Western culture has been due in part to inadequate translation. Polarizing conclusions have resulted in different branches of Christianity that developed over time. It's important to remember when reading Paul's writings that he was addressing the first century church in the first century culture in the first century context. His writings must be understood in the framework of the era in which he lived and the audience he addressed in each of his epistles.

As Paul worked to evangelize and establish churches in the Gentile world, he faithfully interpreted and applied what he had learned from Jesus—the one who came to fulfill the Scripture he had been trained to know from his youth. On the subject of a woman's place in the church, Paul didn't back away from the revolutionary stance Jesus exampled.

SIDENOTE
from Kevin M. Shaw

In my opinion, the argument over whether women may "teach" in a church setting is not solved by discourse analysis. That issue goes to Paul's intended meaning of the words for woman/wife, man/husband, teach, exercise authority, and learn, and quietness.

I can and must obey the first portion of the chapter in real life by praying with all four of the types of prayer Paul mentions. I must obey by praying for persons who are in authority so that the society may be peaceful—and by praying everywhere, lifting up clean hands and heart.

I can live in comportment with the doctrine ... like a true believer. Women can live in obedience to the Word by not bossing their husbands, telling them what to do, "instructing" them, but rather live in quiet submissiveness, and profess and live in godliness ... to continue living in faith and love and holiness, with sensibleness.

> Those wives who refuse to speak the Word publicly but who nonetheless are always telling their husbands what to do are not in alignment with this important passage.
>
> —Kevin M. Shaw
>   Pastor; Denver, Colorado

He had received a transformational revelation from the Lord himself. Jesus capsized the established patriarchal practices of the Jews as surely as he overturned the moneychanger's tables in the temple. Paul and Jesus were both radical, but what Jesus initiated, Paul had the responsibility to organize and apply to the fledgling church.

Some consider Paul a chauvinist, but I believe readers have at times improperly understood his words. While some of his writings are easily misinterpreted by the translations and limitations of our Western understanding, they must be examined for what they truly say and in the light of the larger context of his teachings and example. Twenty-three percent of the New Testament is attributed to Paul's writing—possibly more—and he has been mischaracterized because Christians have misunderstood the deep spiritual concepts he was conveying.

Jesus primarily ministered in Palestine, a drastically different setting and social environment than the Mediterranean culture Paul missionized. This is the culture in which Paul endeavored to introduce the liberty of the gospel. In the Greco-Roman world, Paul was wise enough to respect the cultural differences and attempt to be "all things to all people" (see 1 Cor 9:22). The Mediterranean world was home to both Greeks and Romans. Women in Roman society often had more freedom than Greek women, but in the eyes of the law, all women were considered inferior to men. History records a few Grecian women who attained some acclaim and influence, but they had no legal status of their own. In pagan worship women weren't allowed to teach, but they could hold a position of priestess or prophetess. Also included in the group were Jewish Christians called Judaizers. These converts wanted Gentile believers to conform to the law of Moses—in essence to make Messianic Jews out of Gentile Christians. But Paul believed Jesus had instituted a new covenant. He knew that because Jesus had come, the world was different. In Christ, men and women of every ethnicity and social class could unite in true worship of the one Lord who gave his life to redeem them all.

As Paul attempted to unite the factions of the young church, he faced a plethora of circumstances including pagan practices, unconventional home environments, and controlling marital relationships. As he navigated the issues discussed at large in other chapters of this book, it's clear he continually viewed women with high regard and offered them the opportunity to not only be a part of the church, but to minister in it.

It's doubtful Paul had the slightest inkling his letters would become part of the canon of Scripture. Undeniable inconsistencies exist between what some scholars interpret Paul's letters to mean and what a close study of the original languages and Paul's practices disclose. What he wrote to validate and liberate has been taken by some to mean the exact opposite of what he most likely intended. This champion of women would surely lament any skewing of his words.

In the letters attributed to Paul, he wrote to nine different people or church locations. Of those nine, two cities were deeply entrenched in goddess worship: Corinth, where Aphrodite was worshiped; and Ephesus, where Artemis (also called Diana) was worshiped. These two cities received the letters that contained what some perceive to be Paul's strongest restrictions on women in ministry. This specific pagan element is our key to understanding these verses.

It's important to remember Paul's main goals were to evangelize, make disciples, and establish churches. In doing so, he was careful not to offend when possible. For instance, he told the Galatians that circumcision was unnecessary. He forbade Titus (a leader in the Galatian church) to be circumcised (see Galatians 2:3). But when Paul took Timothy to minister with him, he had the young man circumcised (see Gal 5:2; Acts 16:1–3).

Was Paul talking out of both sides of his mouth? Or was he doing what he felt would create the best conditions for the gospel message to be received? Considering Paul's words and his examples—on the matter of circumcision, for instance—how should a believer today determine his authoritative position on the matter? And whichever position a person may side with, should any individual's personal conclusion be applied to the church universally when it's clear circumcision and uncircumcision were both endorsed in word and deed by the same man?

Paul's words taken in context with his practices reveal he was a man on a mission. He was not duplicitous or double-dealing.

Without compromising biblical principles, the apostle was willing to go beyond requirements and tailor his conduct to meet a need in a specific situation. Circumcising Timothy was not a practice that was endorsed by the church for New Testament believers, but Paul circumcised Timothy to reach the Jews. Silencing women was not a practice Paul endorsed unilaterally, but he silenced the woman teaching in Ephesus to protect the church from false teaching.

Although people have misunderstood and mischaracterized Paul, an examination of his interaction with women reveals his true position. He followed Jesus's example and gave women the opportunity to respond to the gospel and be included in ministry. In fact, his first convert was a woman named Lydia who had gathered with women to pray by a river. The record of Scripture bears out that Paul valued women as his strong, capable co-laborers. He was a friend and advocate of women in the New Testament church.

Early Church History

But ye are a chosen generation, a royal priesthood.
1 Peter 2:9

In contrast to the contemporary culture in which they lived, women in the first century church could participate in both membership and leadership. Some served in prominent roles and ministered side by side with the apostle Paul. As we examined elsewhere in this book, women served as deacons and in the five-fold ministry as apostles, prophets, evangelists, pastors, and teachers. They served under the direct supervision of the apostles and early church leaders who had walked and talked with Jesus Christ. Women of means used their wealth and homes to support the apostles and local congregations. They facilitated and led house churches where both sons and daughters prophesied.

The Bible contains a few isolated verses that appear to conflict with the pattern of female ministerial leadership revealed in the New Testament. However, it's obvious from the record of Scripture, women were allowed to serve in many different capacities, and the church at large accepted these women without question. Scripture offers some clarity and instruction on how women were to learn and minister, but there is no record of a single woman who was forbidden or "sat down" from ministering simply because of her gender.

In addition to the early church history recorded in Acts, Jesus broke the cultural norm in his day. He ministered directly to women, and he allowed them to minister directly to him. Each of the four gospel writers recorded multiple female followers of Jesus, some of whom were specifically noted as having great faith and discernment.

Scripture indicates that both women and men ministered during the apostolic era. History records a trajectory of the diminished influence of women in the church after the New Testament age. What happened in the centuries that followed and the subsequent suppression of the role of women in ministry? Likely, the influence of surrounding cultures pressed into the church. Also to consider are terms like "clergy" and "laity" that were adopted by the church as it grew in organizational structure. While the early church rightly recognized those called to ministerial elder-ship and oversight, the heightened difference between ministry professionals and regular church members may have curbed the participation of believers in ministry.

Spirit-filled women ministered in the early church, but after Emperor Constantine declared Christianity the state religion of the Roman Empire in the early part of the fourth century, the organism of the church was organized into ecclesiastical rulers with governmental positions and rankings. Although this administration may have been created with good intentions, women's roles changed and they didn't fare well in the new organizational structure.

Some women were notable leaders, and history records their authority in the church. During the Middle Ages (between the fall of Rome in 476 A.D. and the onset of the Reformation in the early sixteenth century) the roles of women varied. Two eleventh century women, Queen Emma of Normandy, and Edith, wife of Edward the Confessor, were appointed bishops in the English church.[103]

Boniface, who was considered the "apostle to the Germans," requested women assist him in his work converting the pagan Saxons to Christianity. In the early seventh century, a woman named Fara founded a community of both men and women, where she served as abbess with priestly authority.[104]

Following the Middle Ages, the Reformation splintered the dominant Catholic church in Europe. With its promotion of a "priesthood of all believers," the Reformation made strides in the right direction, but for the most part people held to the inherited philosophy that restricted women from leadership.

Women Martyrs

The early persecution of Christians, specifically Christian women, testifies to the roles they played in ministry. Before his conversion, Saul sought letters approving his mission to capture those found in the way "whether they were men or women, [that] he might bring them bound unto Jerusalem" (see Acts 9:2). Paul arrested both men and women. In his own words, he said, "And I persecuted this way unto the death, binding and delivering into prisons both men and women" (Acts 22:4).

The record of persecution testifies to the fact women were speaking on behalf of the Lord Jesus Christ. And the persecution continued. Pliny the Younger, a lawyer and magistrate of Ancient Rome, used torture to interrogate two female slaves who were called deacons in the church.[105]

Vibia Perpetua, a second century Christian martyr, journaled her trial and imprisonment for her faith. Before her death in the arena she wrote *The Passion of Saints Perpetua and Felicity,* one of the rare surviving texts authored by a woman in the ancient world.[106]

Two third century martyrs lived in Alexandria during a local uprising against Christians. The stories of the women were recorded by Dionysius, the bishop of Alexandria, in his letters to Fabius, the bishop of Antioch. The first, a woman named Quinta, was seized by a pagan mob and carried to their temple. They attempted to force her to worship their idol, but "as she turned away in detestation, they bound her feet and dragged her through the entire city … and at the same time scourged her; then, taking her to the same place, stoned her to death."[107]

The second woman, Appollonia, was considered to be at least a deaconess. She was seized and beaten and ultimately plunged herself into the same fire her persecutors threatened to burn her alive in if she did not repeat their blasphemous words or invoke their heathen gods.[108] Dionysius identified Appollonia as "the *parthénos presbûtis.*" This term is rendered in Latin *virgo presbytera,* or virgin presbytery.[109] *Presbytera* is derived from the Greek word for "priest" which is translated "elder" in the New Testament. Although we do not know this woman's precise role in the church, Appollonia was certainly an esteemed leader who was persecuted and subsequently died for her faith.

In the fourth century, Catherine of Alexandria, a princess and noted scholar, converted to Christianity at the age of 14. She converted hundreds of people to Christianity before being executed for her faith at the age of 18.[110]

Another woman of renown in the early church was Marcella. She was a woman of substance educated in both Greek and Hebrew. Jerome, a fourth century Italian priest and theologian, spent three years in what he called her "domestic church." It was in Marcella's home he translated the Bible into Latin. Marcella not only facilitated and financed the work, but critiqued Jerome's translation and even settled disputes on the interpretation of Scripture.[111] When Marcella was in her late seventies, soldiers stormed her residence. She went to the church in St. Paul for refuge where she died the next day.[112]

This sampling of women who suffered and died for their faith represents only a fraction of women whose stories were not recorded in the annals of history or in Scripture. Silent women would have remained untouched by would-be persecutors. Those who were actively witnessing, teaching, preaching, and leading were identified and persecuted. Their persecution and deaths authenticate the historicity of their ministerial and leadership roles in the early church and throughout the Middle Ages.

Elders, Pastors, Bishops, Shepherds, and Teachers

The roles and responsibilities of elders have varied throughout time and cultures. While history does not record specific duties elders performed in civic realms or faith traditions, archeology has uncovered some vital information. Tombs document the historicity of female Jewish elders.[113] Ancient writings and artifacts also bear witness to women who served as synagogue rulers in several locations. The list includes Rufina of Smyrna, Peristeria of Thebes in Thessaly, Theopempte of Myndos, and Sophia of Gortyn on Crete.[114]

In the New Testament, gospel writers used the Greek word *presbyteros,* translated "elder," in reference to a rank or office among the Jews. These *presbyteros* included the members of the Sanhedrin (the great council) who were selected from among the elderly men. The term was also used for those who managed public affairs and administered justice as well as those who were simply advanced in years.[115]

As the church became established, it adopted titles used by both Jewish and Gentile believers. While qualifications are given for varying roles, the functions and responsibilities of elders are not clearly defined by Scripture. In attempting to structure contemporary church leadership to the biblical model we must first correctly understand what those titles meant to the first century church. This is especially true given that in today's multi-denominational church world ministry roles and job descriptions differ even though they often use the same titles.

The first reference of "elder" in the early church was used to identify men sent on a relief mission to people suffering in another community (see Acts 11:28–30). Prior to this reference, no official position of elder is documented in the church structure. The first reference to a formal elder appointment is found late in the book of Acts. "And when they had ordained them elders in every church, and had prayed with fasting, they commended them to the Lord, on whom they believed" (Acts 14:23). Note the elders were ordained.

The Greek word *presbyteros* translates as both "elder men" and "elder women." In Luke's chronicling of the above verse, he could have employed the word *presbytēs,* a gender-specific term indicating men, but he did not. Considering the text, the ordained *them* should not be exclusively referred to men. The *presbyteros* could have been both "elder men" and "elder women."

Paul specifically mentioned elder women elsewhere in Scripture: "The aged women likewise, that they be in behaviour as becometh holiness, not false accusers, not given to much wine, teachers of good things" (Titus 2:3). In this passage "aged women" is rendered from *presbytis,* the feminine form of the word *presbytēs.* These female elders were called to holy conduct and to be "teachers of good things" in the same way bishops were qualified and instructed in 1 Timothy 3 and elders in Titus 1.

According to Scripture, the primary role of an elder in the church is to provide leadership and oversight—to superintend. In his book *Biblical Eldership,* Alexander Strauch summarized the functions and role of an elder:

> Elders lead the church, teach and preach the Word, protect the church from false teachers, exhort and admonish the saints in sound doctrine, visit the sick and pray, and judge doctrinal issues. In biblical terminology, elders shepherd, oversee, lead, and care for the local church.[116]

There has been confusion concerning the office of elder, bishop, and pastor in biblical times. In the early church these titles were different names for the same office. In Paul's letter to Timothy, the qualifications to hold the office of bishop parallel those he issued to Titus for the office of elder (see 1 Tim 3:1–7; Titus 1:6–9). In fact, Paul wrote Titus instructing him to ordain elders in the same way he had appointed him an elder (see Titus 1:4–5). Paul continued his discussion of elders using the title "bishop" (v. 7). The apostle referred to Titus as both elder and bishop.

The word "pastor" is used only once in the New Testament (see Eph 4:11). It is the Greek word *poimēn* that is translated "shepherd" 17 times elsewhere. In Acts, Paul specifically addressed elders and admonished them to take heed to the flock "over which the Holy Ghost hath made you overseers" (see Acts 20:17, 28). Overseeing and shepherding are considered pastoral duties. Peter called himself an elder and directed other elders to "feed the flock of God" and take "the oversight thereof" (see 1 Pet 5:1–2).

Again, these are pastoral duties assigned to elders. The main responsibilities of a shepherd are to feed, direct, and protect the flock under his or her care. Paul said an elder was to feed the flock "the faithful word as he hath been taught, that he may be able by sound doctrine both to exhort and to convince the gainsayers" (see Titus 1:9.)

The Greek word *episcopē* translates "bishop" and means "overseership." This word is not included in the five-fold ministry (see Eph 4:11). Since "overseeing" the flock is certainly the responsibility of an elder, it seems bishop is also used interchangeably for pastor and elder. Some denominations differentiate between the offices of pastors, bishops, and elders; however, this application does not seem to be reflected in the early church.

A pastor is a shepherd who feeds the church. A pastor is an elder (not necessarily aged, but mature in the faith), and a pastor provides the function of overseeing and leading local congregations. J. B. Lightfoot, a nineteenth century English theologian and author said, "It is a fact now generally recognized by theologians of all shades of opinion, that in the language of the New Testament the same officer in the Church is called indifferently 'bishop [overseer]' (episkopos) and 'elder' or 'presbyter' (presbyteros)."[117]

In some church cultures the office of pastor has been open exclusively to men. It seems, however, after examining this topic, the biblical position of the contemporary church should acknowledge women called to nurture, oversee, and lead the people of God as pastors. Women called and gifted by God to serve in pastoral roles should be eligible for the same ordination, titles, and positions open to men.

God's Chosen Pastor

The responsibility to appoint men and women as pastors and overseers of the church belongs to the Lord who purchased the church with his blood (see Acts 20:28). Paul specified it was by the will of God and appointment of God that he was a preacher, apostle, and teacher (see 2 Tim 1:1; 1:11).

While God is the one who makes a call and appointment, he also puts the desire in the hearts of his chosen. "This is a true saying, if a man desire the office of a bishop, he desireth a good work" (see 1 Tim 3:1).

The word rendered "man" in the King James Version of this verse is the Greek *ei tis,* which is also rendered "if any" elsewhere in Scripture and implies no gender. If *ei tis* referred exclusively to men, a consistent masculine rendering would mean only men are required to pick up their crosses and follow the Lord (see Matt 16:24) and only men are eligible to have the Spirit of God dwell in them (see Rom 8:9). Context must be considered to correctly interpret the meaning in this passage which will be discussed in more detail in the pages ahead.

Some confuse the new covenant office of pastor with the Old Testament role of priest, but Scripture is clear. The Old Testament priestly function of offering sacrifices was replaced with the sacrifice of Jesus (see Heb 10:12–14). A new covenant was made, and there are no more offerings made for sin (see Heb 10:16–19). Each individual believer goes to the Lord for forgiveness of his or her trespasses. Comparing the New Testament role of pastor to the Old Testament Jewish role of priest is simply an apples-to-oranges comparison.

Pastoring includes an element of "ruling," but never for self. In fact a pastor's authority is limited by the Word to the role of shepherding the people of God. A shepherd guides and leads his or her congregation in the will of God with love and patience and with the goal of helping others grow in spiritual health and maturity.

Men and women bring different gifts to the ministry table. In *Men Are Like Waffles— Women Are Like Spaghetti,* authors Bill and Pam Farrel offer a vivid illustration of how the natures of men and women differ. They propose men are like waffles (each element of their lives has its own separate box) while women are more like spaghetti (everything in their lives touches everything else). Men and women may approach pastoral ministry with similar goals and equal abilities but with manners and methods that differ. Men and women input, process, and deliver information differently.

> ## SIDENOTE
> ### *from Mark Jordan*
>
> People grant enormous influence over their lives to trusted leaders. Each minister needs to guard against any temptation to wrongly use this power. The minister's authority is not absolute.... Nowhere does the Bible give broad, sweeping authority to any minister over the souls in his care.[168]
>
> —J. Mark Jordan
> Former Superintendent, Ohio District United Pentecostal Church

While there are exceptions, for the most part women tend to be more personal than men and more intent on building relationships. This is where the gentler side of shepherding often gets pushed into a corner. When the male perspective dominates a local church body or organization, church leadership can get off-balance. A woman's potential insights and gifts may remain untapped and/or underutilized. Her approach to administration and problem solving could greatly enhance the church. What God has given to benefit the body of Christ at large should be broadly shared in the work of the Lord. Men and women serving side by side bring the fullness of God's nature in the church.

Deacons

Organization and offices have evolved since the New Testament was written. From the first century on, the church developed structure as it went along. As with the terms "elder" and "pastor," to correctly apply the meaning of the word "deacon" requires looking beyond modern-day usage to the word's meaning in the early church.

The apostles who walked with Jesus were the church's first leaders. Jesus taught them. He discipled them in "the way." After his ascension, these leaders received on-the-job training when it came to developing the structure and organization of the rapidly growing church. The church is a living organism, and as it grew new issues came to the fore that resulted in new procedures being implemented. Dealing with these issues not only affirmed the leadership of the original disciples, it expanded leadership to others. If not, the work of the church would have died out with the Twelve Apostles.

The Greek word *diakoneō* is translated five times in the New Testament with specific reference to the office of "deacon." The same Greek word is elsewhere rendered "minister" or "servant" twenty-eight times. As discussed previously, Paul used the word *diakoneō* when he commended Phebe's ministry.

The Greek word translated "deacon" is also rendered "serve" in Acts 6. The incident recorded in this chapter is commonly accepted as the first record of deacons in the church. While some have limited the function of deacons to attending to physical needs like those of the widows, the word also means the following:

"wait upon (menially or as a host, friend, or (figuratively) teacher);

technically, to act as a Christian deacon:

—(ad-)minister (unto), serve, use the office of a deacon."[119]

The first deacons served tables, but their ministry included more than distributing food. They would have managed all the resources for the widows provided by the church. These first deacons alleviated the busy work of the apostles by tending to the widows' physical needs. They were also mightily used in other areas. Stephen's message recorded in the chapter following his appointment as a deacon is one of the most dynamic presentations of the overall plan of God in the written Word.

The church was growing, and Peter realized that to continue the spread of the gospel and the ongoing expansion of the church, responsibility and power must be delegated to others. When selecting the first deacons,

> **Serving is a verb. Deacon is a verb. The office of deacon implies active service in the body of Christ in whatever capacity is needed.**

Peter chose from those who were already being used and had a good reputation.

Meeting a person's physical needs (when done in Jesus's name) is a spiritual activity. Jesus set the example. He met physical needs while ministering to souls. The ministry of serving tables in no way hampered the first deacons' ministries. In fact, as a result of Peter empowering the seven to serve, the men appointed were lifted to positions of prominence. Their acts of service may well have launched them into new ministry opportunities. As mentioned, Stephen gained eternal renown as a remarkable preacher. Philip later became an incredible, Holy-Spirit-teleported evangelist (see Acts 8:26–40). What a precedent they set!

Qualifications

First Timothy 3:8–12 is the only passage that specifically outlines the qualifications for the office of deacon. This may not be an exhaustive list, but notice its focus is not on duties, but on spiritual maturity and reputation. According to a straight-forward reading in English of Paul's letter, below are the qualifications for deacons:

1. Grave: of honorable character and deeds, respectable
2. *Not* double-tongued: saying one thing with one person, and then something else to another with the intent to deceive; two-faced, insincere, lacking credibility

3. *Not* given to much wine: addicted to intoxicating substances; lacking self-control
4. *Not* greedy of filthy lucre: eager for gain, a lover of money
5. Holding the mystery of the faith in a pure conscience: continuing in the gospel—the truths of God—in both beliefs and conduct
6. Proved: tested and found to be genuine
7. Blameless: of irreproachable character, unaccused, having a clean track record of service
8. Grave wives: a spouse of honorable character and deeds, respectable, who live out the same morality and faith as their husbands
9. Husband of one wife: faithful, a "one-woman man" who is not connected emotionally or physically with another woman
10. Ruling their children and their own houses well: maintaining and caring for their families.

Points eight and nine above lead to a question, "Why discuss the role of deacons in a book about women in ministry when the biblical qualifications indicate a deacon must be a man?"

The points come from these verses:

"Even so must their wives be grave, not slanderers, sober, faithful in all things. Let the deacons be the husbands of one wife, ruling their children and their own houses well" (1 Tim 3:11–12).

The first verse begins with the Greek word translated "even so." This word is also translated "likewise" in this unit of teaching addressed to deacons and is translated "in like manner" earlier in the same chapter (see 1 Tim 2:9, 3:8). Paul was outlining responsibilities of leadership and the use of this specific word bridged the discussion of one group of leaders with another.

What was the topic of Paul's conversation before he used the word that means "likewise" or "in like manner?" It was men serving as deacons. As Paul outlined the qualifications, he shifted his focus from men to women. He stated that in the same way the men deacons are to conduct themselves, the *gynē* should also conduct themselves.

Gynē, depending on context, can be rendered either "wife" or "woman." The word "their" is simply not in the original text. The writing was not about women in "their" relationship to men. This phrase should more accurately be translated, "Even so, women...."

In Linda Belleville's examination of 1 Timothy in the *Cornerstone Biblical Commentary,* she recorded the words of Clement of Alexandria who "understood this to be to women ministers and not ministers wives: 'We know what the honorable Paul in one of his letters to Timothy prescribed regarding women deacons.'"[120]

Bible scholar Dr. Charles J. Ellicott said, "The position of this solitary charge, respecting deacons' wives, in the midst of regulations concerning 'deacons,' is, of itself almost decisive against the translation of the English version, adopted also by Luther and many other."[121] Ellicott believed the English rendering of "wives" simply did not make sense in this list of regulations for ministers. He made the point that in this same chapter there was no reference made to the character of a bishop (overseer) who holds higher position in the church. If a man's wife had no bearing on the selection of a bishop, why would this matter concern Timothy when selecting deacons?

Ellicott's commentary further stated, "The literal translation of the Greek words would be, *Women in like manner must,* &c. these *women,* St. Chrystostom and most of the ancient expositors affirm, were *deaconesses.*"[122]

The biblical record affirms women did hold official positions in the early church (see Rom 16:1, Phil 4:2). Ellicott cited a Professor Reynolds regarding deaconesses in the Western church who said, "the order did not cease to exist until the fifth century, and was continued in the Greek Church till the twelfth. The deaconess vanished into the cloister until partially revived in comparatively modern times."[123]

From this perspective Paul's instructions in verse 11 were not meant to prevent women from serving as deacons because they were female. He was specifying qualifications similar to those the men must meet.

Women deacons are to be:

1. Grave: of honorable character and deeds, respectable, who live out the same morality and faith as their spouses
2. Not slanderers: spreading malicious, false reports
3. Sober: temperate, abstaining from wine (from a root word that means watchful)
4. Faithful in all things: trustworthy in everything

The structure of Paul's writing indicates that he was empowering Timothy to select women to serve in the leadership of the church where he served as bishop. Considering that Paul lay the foundations for the Ephesian church with Priscilla and Aquila, this seems reasonable and logical.

The next verse in the chapter deals specifically with spouses:

"Let the deacons be the husbands of one wife, ruling their children and their own houses well" (1 Tim 3:12). At first reading, this verse could complicate the discussion, but does it indicate that only married men with children are eligible to serve as deacons? Could not widowers? Single men? Men who before coming to Christ had been divorced or had more than one marriage partner?

Certainly the meaning of this passage is important to believers today. More important was its meaning to Paul when he wrote it and what his readers understood it to mean. Taken on its own merit this verse would disqualify the very person who wrote it (who served at an even higher level of apostolic leadership) as well as the single man he was writing to. Neither Paul nor Timothy would have been eligible to serve in the lesser office of deacon.

In a society where polygamy was practiced, it's likely Paul included this statement to emphasize marital fidelity. A male deacon should have one wife, and conversely a woman in leadership should have only one husband. Paul discussed this issue elsewhere when he spoke to the fidelity of women (see 1 Tim 5:9). Marital faithfulness was expected from both men and women.

The final qualification was "ruling well" whatever size "house" a deacon might have. Whether a person is married, single, widowed, or childless, a deacon should manage his or her home and provide well for the household.

Jesus elevated serving to the highest place of honor (see Mark 10:43–45). Serving others over self was a fundamental teaching of Jesus and an essential part of a disciple's character (see Luke 22:26). Each of the four gospels gives accounts of women serving alongside Jesus. In reference to these women, three of the gospel writers specifically used the word *diakonia* which is translated elsewhere as "deacon" (see Matt 27:55–57; Mark 15:40; Luke 23:49).

In *The Role of Women in Ecclesial Ministry,* Agnes Cunningham recorded historical sources and church documents from the third century that evidence females serving in the office of deaconess.[124] Among them were the *Apostolic Constitutions* and the *Didascalia Apostolorum,* considered to be the earliest reliable evidence to the office of female deacons. It is notable, however, the term "deaconess" is never used in Scripture, only "deacon" which is a masculine/feminine noun.

Cunningham wrote, "In the *Apostolic Constitutions* we learn that a deaconess was 'a pure virgin or at least a widow who had been but once married, faithful and well esteemed.'"[125] She went on to say, "The compiler locates deaconesses properly within all the categories of membership and functions within the church."[126] According to these ancient church documents, some women were appointed and ordained. Even in a patriarchal church culture, women were officially recognized and authorized to serve in leadership.

The Bible does not outline the specific functions of deacons. These have evolved since the first appointment of those who served the widows (see Acts 6). Early deacons may or may not have had official teaching roles. While qualifications for elders included being "apt to teach," deacons were instructed only to continue "holding" to the faith (see 1 Tim 3:2, 9).

Times have changed and church practices along with them. Independent churches and church organizations have the liberty to define the function of deacons in their frameworks. The primary role of a deacon from a biblical perspective should be to free spiritual leadership to shepherd and teach the people. This will look different in different church environments.

SIDENOTE *from Doug Klinedinst*

Spiritual authority goes far beyond positional authority or a hierarchal structure in the body of Christ. Each and every believer has the opportunity to receive and function in spiritual authority. This dimension of spiritual authority does not negate or supersede positional authority, but rather operates in harmony with established spiritual government.

To understand this kind of spiritual authority, a different definition is helpful. Authority in this context is best described as expertise, knowledge, skill, or capability. These attributes are provided to the individual believer through the anointing of the Holy Ghost, disciplined study, and years of experience.

The Word and the Spirit of God give believers divine authorization. The great commission recorded in Mark 16:15–18 includes preaching the gospel, laying hands on the sick for healing, and casting out demons.

There are times when gifting must submit to positional authority. There are times when positional authority will yield to gifting. Skillful, experienced pillars in the church will provide direction and release to those who are receiving gifting and anointing through prayer, fasting, and study of the Word.[127]

—Douglas C. Klinedinst
International Evangelist, Mentor, and Author; Ocala, Florida

A Nineteenth and Twentieth Century Historical Overview

But ye are a chosen generation, a royal priesthood, an holy nation,
a peculiar people; that ye should shew forth the praises of him who hath
called you out of darkness into his marvellous light.
1 Peter 2:9

In Chapter 7 we looked at the duties and functions of men and women in ministry in the early church and how they changed over the years following. In this chapter we will examine the roles women played in key revivals that took place in the nineteenth and twentieth centuries.

The Holiness Movement

Women played key roles in the Holiness Movement, a religious movement that arose among Protestant churches in the nineteenth century that emphasized a doctrine of sanctification. Phoebe Palmer is considered one of the movement's founders. She began missions (including the first inner-city mission in New York City) and evangelized at camp meetings. Through her personal ministry in North America and Europe, 25,000 people turned their hearts to the Lord.[128] In 1859, she published *The Promise of the Father*, a book in favor of women in ministry.

Frances Willard, one of the founders of the Women's Christian Temperance Union, evangelized alongside Dwight L. Moody to audiences numbering in the thousands.[129] Her work in obtaining the vote for women was based on her interpretation of Scripture.[130] She said, "God sets male and female side by side throughout his realm of law."[131]

Hannah Whitehall-Smith was an evangelist and influential woman in the Holiness Movement. She "was known as 'the angel of the churches' both for her eloquence and for her appearance in her evangelistic addresses to huge gatherings."[132] The publication of her best-selling book, *The Christian's Secret of a Happy Life,* coincided with the impact of her preaching in Britain and Continental Europe. In Oxford she preached to 7,000, and her congregation was larger than Charles Spurgeon's.[133]

Catherine Booth co-founded the Salvation Army with her husband, General William Booth. An integral leader and dynamic speaker, she championed the cause of women in ministry, even persuading her husband who was initially not a supporter. In 1859, she wrote a brief but powerful book, *Female Ministry: Women's Right to Preach the Gospel.* Catherine had her own evangelistic itinerary. She was the breadwinner of the family. Her preaching earned more money than her husband's.[134] General William Booth, who was one of the most powerful Christian leaders of the nineteenth century, summed up his views on women in ministry when he said, "Some of my best men are women!"[135]

While women were hindered from serving in some churches, they were commonly allowed to minister in many of the denominations of the Holiness movement. Edith Blumhofer, PhD in American Religious History, noted that in the early days of Pentecostalism "having the 'anointing' was far more important than one's sex ... women who were recognized as having the anointing of the Holy Spirit shared with men in preaching ministry."[136] She went on to say, "A person's call—and how other believers viewed it—was far more important than [ministerial credentials]."[137]

Azusa Street Revival

The Pentecostal renewal at the turn of the twentieth century began on January 1, 1901, when Agnes Ozman first received the infilling of the Holy Spirit with the evidence of speaking in tongues. It happened at Bethel Bible College in Topeka, Kansas, run by Charles Parham and his wife Sarah. According to James L. Tyson, author of *The Early Pentecostal Revival,* Brother and Sister Parham were "both doing the work of saving souls, curing the sick, and turning out crops of new evangelists from their Bible school."[138]

It was just after midnight on the first day of the twentieth century when Agnes Ozman made a request to Charles Parham. According to Parham, Ozman "asked that hands might be laid upon her to receive the Holy Spirit as she hoped to go to foreign fields. Glory fell upon her."[139]

The release of the Spirit of God in that Bible college prayer meeting proved to be a harbinger of the Azusa Street Revival that would follow in 1906. Parham was one of two central figures in the early Pentecostal revival. William Seymour was the second. Seymour became involved through a woman who connected him with a work in Los Angeles. He was invited to pastor a small mission church, but after he preached his first sermon from the book of Acts, he was informed that his services would not be needed.

Seymour was padlocked out of the church by its leadership, but then invited to stay in the home of one of its members, Edward S. Lee. Some of the members of the mission church attended Bible studies and prayer meetings at Lee's house on Bonnie Brae Street. People began receiving the Holy Spirit, including Seymour and the woman he would eventually marry. The gatherings were so well attended the worshippers moved to a new location on the same street, and not long after to a much larger building on Azusa Street.

Men, women, and children from all walks of life experienced the infilling of the Spirit of God. People from varying denominations came together including blacks, whites, Hispanics, and Asians. The rich worshipped alongside the poor. The educated knelt beside the illiterate in humble devotion united as brothers and sisters in Christ.

The revival broke out during the peak of the "Jim Crow" racial segregation and fourteen years before women obtained the right to vote on a national scale.[140] The amalgamation of these diverse people was indeed a remarkable work of God. The Azusa Street Mission was a place people laid down their pride and their prejudices. American Pentecostal writer Frank Bartleman said that at the mission, "The religious ego preached its own funeral sermon quickly."[141]

The emphasis in the meetings was not speaking in tongues, but experiencing God. Spiritually hungry people came from around the world seeking to know Jesus in a deeper and higher way. They received the gift of the spirit of God, and then returned to their homes and mission fields to share their experiences with others.

There is something that happens during a revival. As hearts ignite with the fire of God, prejudices burn away. In the early days at the Azusa Street mission, ministry was accepted by all and from all. After times of prayer, in an atmosphere thick with the presence of God, either a man or woman would stand and deliver an anointed word. Even children were allowed to speak. In the early days of the revival both men and women served in its leadership. In fact, when William Seymour passed away in 1922, his wife Jennie became the pastor of their church.

Following are some highlights of women who served in the ministry and leadership of the Pentecostal revival.

- In 1903, Charles Parham prayed with a woman named Mary Arthur who received a physical healing and the gift of the Holy Spirit. She subsequently opened her home in Galena, Kansas, and invited Parham there to preach. The meeting grew to be a three-month revival that was so well attended it moved to a large tent. Hundreds of lives were touched and 250 people received the Holy Spirit. As a result of the revival, Mary Arthur and her friend, Francene Dobson, founded a permanent Apostolic Faith mission. It was the first organized Pentecostal church in North America and became the spiritual home of Howard Goss. Goss was saved in the Galena revival and later became the first Superintendent of the United Pentecostal Church International.
- In 1906, Marie Burgess met Charles Parham and converted to Pentecostalism. She preached in the Midwest and then in New York City, where she founded a mission called Glad Tidings Hall. After her marriage to Robert Brown, she and her husband established Glad Tidings Tabernacle. Their church became a hub in spreading revival in the Eastern United States, and after her husband's passing, Marie continued to pastor on her own for 23 years.
- In 1906, several ladies began traveling ministries. Florence Crawford, Mabel Smith, Ivey Campbell, Millicent McClendon, and Rachel Sizelove were among many who traveled and preached. These women spread Pentecostal revival wherever they ministered.
- In 1906, Ellen Hebden became the first known person in Canada to receive the gift of the Holy Spirit. Following the experience, the Hebden Mission she and her husband founded became a center for the early Pentecostal revival in Canada.
- In 1907, Emma Ladd transformed a local rescue mission into a powerhouse of Pentecostalism. She was the wife of a popular Iowan Supreme Court Justice, and her ministry made such an impact a warrant was issued for her arrest.
- In Rochester, New York, Hattie Duncan and her sisters operated the Elim Faith Home. Originally founded in 1895, this work published a journal, established a church, and founded the Rochester Training School for Missions. The sisters heard about the Pentecostal outpouring and received it for themselves in 1907. In the wake of that experience, the school became

a training ground for Pentecostal leaders including over 400 missionaries. The school promoted the Pentecostal message and became famous for the healings that occurred there.[142]

- Florence L. Crawford established the Apostolic Faith Mission in Portland, Oregon. Over time this work became the hub from which other Northwest missions works turned for leadership. It was from this mission "the first Pentecostal missionaries were dispatched to the foreign fields, as early as 1907 or 1908."[143]

- In 1908, the Duncan sisters and Mary Leanore Barnes, along with Mary's son-in-law, B. F. Lawrence, conducted tent meetings in southern Illinois. Mary became known as "Mother Barnes" and taught at a Bible school in Eureka Springs, Arkansas.

- In 1908, the Pentecostal Assemblies of the World met and elected a woman identified as Sister Hopkins as temporary chairman.[144]

- In 1913, at the worldwide camp meeting in Arroyo Secco, California, Maria Woodworth-Etter was the featured evening speaker. Woodworth-Etter's ministry and involvement with the Holiness Movement earned her the title "grandmother of the Pentecostal movement." She established twelve churches and was responsible for licensing ministers. This prominent Pentecostal leader founded the Woodworth-Etter Tabernacle in 1918 which she pastored until her passing in 1924. An active evangelist, Maria spoke to crowds of over twenty-five thousand "while hundreds fell to the ground under the power of God."[145]

- In 1923, Evangelist Aimee Semple McPherson founded the International Church of the Foursquare Gospel. She was the first woman in history to preach over the radio, and in 1924, she established KSFG, one of the first Christian radio stations in the United States.[146]

- From 1924 to 1951, Sister Hilda Reeder led in early foreign missions work that she launched under the ministry of G.T. Haywood, Bishop of the Pentecostal Assemblies of the World (PAW). At the time of her appointment, Reeder served as the only female member of the PAW's Executive Board.[147]

- In the late 1920s, groundwork was laid for what would eventually become the PAW's Sunday School Association. Included in their leadership were Sister Willa B. Howard and Sister Mary Johnson.[148]

Women played significant roles in the rise and spread of the Pentecostal movement. The free move of the spirit of God upon both males and females nullified societal norms.

Men and women, sons and daughters, heard God's voice and spoke forth the words he gave them with boldness and authority. The historical record of this movement clearly details women called of God who served in the forefront as leaders, preachers, evangelists, and missionaries, as well as Bible school founders and instructors.

After Azusa

Following the great revival that spread from Azusa Street and the formation of a more formal church structure, the roles of women in ministry began to change. The shift took place over time and after several decades of notable ministry by powerful women of God.

In 1914, one third of the Assemblies of God ministers were women and two thirds of their missionaries. In the earliest oneness Pentecostal minister's directory published in 1919, of the 704 names listed, 29 percent of the credentialed ministers were women.

What happened to these great moves of God that changed the status of women who were once welcomed to participate in ministry and leadership? One factor could be that once a move of God was launched and began to organize, women were often displaced by men or deliberately became less active and accepted lesser positions. When church structures became formalized, the roles women previously served in active leadership and ministry were either designated to men or abdicated by well-intentioned women.

In 1980, Charles H. Barfoot and Gerald T. Sheppard wrote a paper on the changing role of women in clergy. In it they said, "As routinization and regimentation of community relationships set in, reactions did occur against the [Pentecostal] movement's prophesying daughters."[149] It seems the primary factor for the change had to do with the subject of authority.

As Pentecostal churches developed, something shifted. Previously women had been free to function according to their calls, character, and giftings, but with structure came restriction. People began to take issue with women as authority figures—a concept that was not seen in the early days of the Pentecostal revival, as recorded by eye-witness Frank Bartleman. He said, "All obeyed God in meekness and humility. In honor we 'preferred one another.' The Lord was liable to burst through any one ... It might be a child, a woman, or a man."[150]

In 2007, Eric Patterson and Edmund Rybarczyk wrote in "The Future of Pentecostalism in the United States" their shared belief that the roles of women were affected by a variety of influences. "Over the years, the proportion of women ministers and pastors [in Oneness Pentecostalism] has diminished greatly." They report their findings based primarily on three factors:

1. An increase in the number of men who entered the movement and the ministry
2. The influence of Fundamentalism and evangelicalism
3. A backlash against the women's liberation movement of the 1960s and 1970s.[151]

Patterson and Rybarczyk also said, "Pentecostal women did not want to be seen as rebellious or radical…. Sometimes a woman maintained the primary role of preaching while her husband sought ministerial license as well. In many cases, women … married ministers and worked alongside their husbands without seeking credentials."[152]

The authors noted a recent resurgence in Pentecostal churches of encouragement and affirmation for women in ministry. They wrote that in the United Pentecostal Church International, although top positions of leadership continue to be reserved for men, the organization "has always allowed the ordination of women" and "there have been calls for greater affirmation of women in ministry."[153]

The History of
Women in Ministry

*Contributed by David K. Bernard, General Superintendent
of the United Pentecostal Church International*

In the earliest directory of Apostolic Pentecostal ministers, from 1919, 29 percent of the ministers were women. At the formation of the United Pentecostal Church in 1945, 21 percent of the credentialed ministers were women, including our first general superintendent's wife.

There has been a decline since then. One reason was that Apostolic women did not want to identify with the unbiblical values of the secular women's liberation movement. Another reason was the influence of Fundamentalism, a conservative reaction to liberal Protestants who denied the infallibility of Scripture. Fundamentalists emphasized the Bible as the Word of God but did not believe in miracles for today. The early Pentecostals also reacted against Protestant liberalism, but they emphasized a revival of the Spirit in addition to the Word.

Early Pentecostals did not have written theology, so they often looked to other conservative groups such as the Fundamentalists for study materials and training tools. The Fundamentalists opposed women preachers based on a limited analysis of two biblical texts in 1 Corinthians 14 and 1 Timothy 2, without considering the complete literary and historical context, the other writings of Paul, examples in the rest of Scripture, and the history of the Holiness-Pentecostal movement. Instead of borrowing theology from others, if we go back to our roots in the New Testament church and in the early Pentecostal movement we find an active role for women in ministry.

In church history, when revival movements emphasized the anointing and gifts of the Spirit, then women's roles were recognized. When churches focused mostly on institutional ministry, then women's roles declined. During the third century, churches became more formal with less emphasis on the Spirit, and the institutional church did not give full recognition to the ministry of women.

In the Pentecostal movement, we appreciate structure but recognize the dangers of institutionalism. The hallmark of our movement is that every generation must go back to the first century and be renewed. In other words, we are restorationists. One thing that every generation should restore is the role of women in ministry. In the last decade, we have seen a significant increase in the number of credentialed women ministers in the United Pentecostal Church International. While the percentage is not as great, we now have more women ministers in the UPCI than ever before.

For further discussion, see David K. Bernard, *The Apostolic Church in the Twenty-first Century.*

Licensing, Ordination and Offices in the Church

And the things you have heard me say in the presence of many witnesses entrust to reliable people who will also be qualified to teach others.
2 Timothy 2:2

The church of Jesus Christ is an organism made of equally valuable people. In it, the Lord established leadership to provide structure and oversight. Jesus painted his ideal for the church as one in which all members loved, served, and mutually submitted to one another—preferring one another in love. This was a "new wine" concept that could not be poured into the "old wineskin" of the Jewish religious establishment (see Mark 2:21–22). The church was birthed to function as a body.

In the early days of the church people met at different locations, primarily in homes. All the believers in a city, however, were regarded as members of one, city-wide church. This is evidenced by the instructions in some of Paul's letters. He wrote one letter "to all that be in Rome," and within the body of the letter he addressed more than one company of believers (see Rom 1:7, 16:5, 15–16). These churches led their own local affairs while maintaining a cooperation and accountability to one another. When the issue of circumcision,

SIDENOTE
from J. T. Pugh

The Christian ministry derives authority from Jesus Christ.... It was a new device for the propagation of the faith that He came to establish in the earth.[154]

—J. T. Pugh
Pastor and Author; Odessa, Texas

for example, was raised in Antioch and in Galatia, elders and apostles met in Jerusalem. Among the leaders gathered, Peter, James, Paul, Barnabas, Judas, and Silas were specifically named. The council discussed the issue, came to agreement on how to handle it, and then issued an official decree (see Acts 15).

The scriptural term "elders" often used for local church leaders is a plural word that indicates shared governmental oversight. In Peter's instructions to church elders, he told those serving they should not act as "lords over God's heritage." Instead, he charged them to be "examples to the flock" (see 1 Pet 5:3).

In the first century church, apostles gave direction to the works they established, but no one person held an authoritarian position over all believers or churches. Leaders were expected to work in harmony and council in their local assemblies. In fact, Jesus taught his disciples that when a disagreement arose, the people involved should attempt to handle it themselves. If that didn't work, then the church was to evaluate the situation and determine the course of action needed (see Matt 18:15–20). Jesus, who was our perfect example, spoke and taught with authority, but he also wrapped a towel around his waist and washed his disciples' feet. The Lord exemplified humility and servant leadership.

Church leadership was designed by God to provide oversight to believers who were called to surrender themselves one to another under the authority of the Word of God. Implementing organizational structure brought order and accountability while it offered respect to the diverse roles and giftings in the body. In the framework established, believers were allowed to function in their gifts and callings for the building up of the church.

This concept contrasts the dominance hierarchy exhibited in nature. A chicken pen is a living example of dominance hierarchy. Hens from the first batch rule the roost, and of those, one is clearly the sovereign fowl. Each spring new chicks are added to the little community, and the new ones quickly learn their places in the pecking order.

In human organizations, hierarchy is established and maintained by a few members who hold rank over other members who submit to the ones in charge. This may work in the corporate world, in politics, and law enforcement (among the "Gentiles"), but it's not God's desire for his church and goes beyond the biblical guidelines of church leadership. Unlike hierarchies that promote individuals to leadership based on lineage, race, gender, social status, or prominence, the church was designed to function on the basis of God-given calls, gifts, and the authority of the Word.

Jesus went to the cross to restore relationships horizontally and vertically. He is the head of his church, and all infrastructure should come under his leadership. The Lord's ministry was punctuated with teachings that repealed old ways of doing things. He lay a new foundation for the church to build its structure upon (see 1 Cor 3:11). He sat his disciples together and said, "If any man desire to be first, the same shall be last of all, and servant of all" (Mark 9:35).

While certainly anointing and authority flow down from God, a leader is a lifter of others. A leader sees him or herself as servant of all—not from a superior position, but one of humility. Leadership in God's church is not as much about rank or office as it is position. Those who would lead in the Lord's church are positioned in places of service.

Jesus said, "Be not ye called Rabbi: for one is Your Master, even Christ; and all ye are brethren" (Matt 23:8). In this statement, the Lord affirmed the point that there was only one Master—and that was him. He was not advocating that all are equally educated or mature or that new converts should be allowed to teach doctrine to elders. He was speaking of seeking title or prominence.

Every disciple of Christ is equally a brother or sister under the Lord's directorship. This concept contrasted the Jewish culture that venerated patriarchs as fathers and put "learners" in subordinate positions to teachers. In reference to church leadership, Jesus said to call no man "father" (see Matt 23:9). In the same context, neither should one call another "master" (see Matt 23:10).

From the list of *don'ts* in Matthew 23 comes the instruction to *do*. Jesus said, "He that is greatest among you shall be your servant. And whosoever shall exalt himself shall be abased; and he that shall humble himself shall be exalted" (see Matt 23:11–12). Jesus implied that those who think they should be esteemed with titles and position (such as Rabbi, Father, or Master) would be demeaned. Those, however, who humble themselves would become great.

The greatest in God's kingdom are not those who promote themselves, but those who teach and preach the words of "The Teacher." They surrender themselves to the person, the timing, and the purposes of God.

Christ-followers are to honor those chosen by God who serve and invest their lives in ministry. One person, however, should not be revered or have absolute authority in the church. This is not the template designed by Jesus and implemented in the New Testament church. Keep in mind a position doesn't automatically produce spiritual authority. An election or appointment to office doesn't of itself impart anointing. Rather, it's the anointing already active in a believer's life that opens the door for greater ministry opportunities.

As the early church grew, the need for organizational structure expanded. People qualified to lead, teach, counsel, and problem-solve were recognized and utilized in their areas of giftedness and calling. Those who labored to plant churches saw the seedling works grounded as they submitted themselves "one to another in the fear of God" (see Eph 5:21).

After the passing of the apostles, over time and with the establishment of a more formalized governmental structure, the sense of community leadership diminished and authority slipped back into a patriarchal and hierarchal order. Specific ceremonies and rituals were implemented that delegated those who were approved to teach, preach, and lead. The formal rituals and new regulations created an environment in some cases in which women were bypassed as possible ministerial candidates. The more formal the church structure, often the less opportunity women were given.

Church Government

Ephesians 4:11 outlines the primary governmental ministries in the New Testament church: "And he gave some, apostles; and some, prophets; and some, evangelists; and some, pastors and teachers." This statement is not a stand-alone verse. It is part of Paul's run-on sentence that doesn't end until verse 16. Together these verses state the purpose of the ministry is to prepare other believers for ministry and to build the church. In this unit of Scripture Paul outlined the basics of church government and then specified that what he had worked to establish according to the Lord's instructions should continue until everyone in the church was fully Christ-like, mature, and stable—grown up in all things and working together.

In another of Paul's letters he further outlined the functions of leadership in the church. "And God hath set some in the church, first apostles, secondarily prophets, thirdly teachers, after that miracles, then gifts of healings, helps, governments, diversities of tongues" (1 Cor 12:28). In Romans, he listed gifts of prophecy, ministry, teaching, exhorting, giving, ruling, and mercy (see Rom 6:8). God supplied his church with the ministry and gifts necessary for it to thrive and grow.

Government of every kind includes directing, managing, and ruling. Every organization has some form of government. In her book *A Woman's Place in God's Government,* Rev. Sharon Walston explained how government functions differently in civic, home, and church environments. The structure of each is unique.[155]

In civic government women serve as mayors, senators, representatives, and presidential cabinet members. They work to write laws and set national policies. Female police officers issue citations and make arrests. Female judges impose fines, community service, and prison sentences. Female governors can stay execution orders, and women are eligible for the highest office in the land.

In families the Lord established a governmental order in which a husband serves as head. This ideal does not work in every situation, however, such as with single women, widows, or in single-parent families. God's family structure was designed to be implemented in a loving environment of mutual respect that exemplifies the relationship Christ would have with his church.

The church is comprised of both men and women who "in Christ" are neither male nor female. The nature of a human is found in the union of a body, soul, and spirit. The human soul and spirit are housed in gendered bodies, but Scripture indicates the eternal souls of the children of God are "equal unto" the angels (see Luke 20:34–36), and angelic beings are genderless (see Heb 2:16). The point is this: in the spiritual realm, there is no gender. That is why human men can become part of the bride of Christ.

While believers look forward to the transformational moment they will become like Jesus, the "kingdom of heaven" is more than a future happening. For those who are in Christ, it is also here and now. The kingdom of heaven was in the midst of the people when Jesus walked the earth, and it is currently within believers who are filled with his Spirit. Christianity goes beyond an experience that simply brings sinners into the kingdom. It establishes them as members of the priesthood of all believers.

The New Testament references priests and priesthoods in three areas:

1. The Levitical Jewish priesthood (see Matt 2:4)
2. Jesus as the great High Priest (see Heb 3:1)
3. The priesthood of all believers (see 1 Pet 2:9, Rev 5:10).

The only priesthood Jesus established was a priesthood in which all could participate. In this priesthood, Jesus is the only mediator (see 1 Tim 2:5), and every believer offers his or her own gifts and sacrifices to the Lord.

In the structure of the New Testament church, apostles took a leading organizational role. Prophets gave guidance and vision. Evangelists gathered in the harvest. Pastors/elders guarded, protected, and fed the local assemblies, and teachers grounded the church in the truths of the Word. Each of these ministry roles or offices is important and was designed by God to work in cooperation with the other ministry gifts for the church to operate in the full dynamic of its power. Together these ministry roles create the framework the Spirit of God flows through. And this framework is not restricted by gender. Biblical and historical records testify that women have successfully served in many church leadership roles throughout the ages.

David K. Bernard wrote on the subject of women in ministry, "Currently [in the UPCI], several key offices are restricted to males.... Other key offices are open to women.... The reason for these distinctions appears to be more cultural and historical than theological."[156]

Licensing and Ordination

Many women who faithfully perform the work of God never seek ministry credentials. Licensing and ordination are not for everyone—men or women. Individual believers must prayerfully determine if ministry credentials would help them serve the church in accordance with their gifts and unique call of God.

A ministry license is a license to serve and can at times be beneficial. Credentials do more than validate a person's ministry within a church. They open doors outside as well. One godly woman who serves as a pastor's wife and ministers internationally was recently denied access to visit a church member in the hospital due to her lack of ministerial credentials. A license would have literally opened the door for her to minister in the restricted area of the hospital. Within

> ### SIDENOTE
> ### *from the Author*
>
> When I began speaking at youth events and ladies' conferences, obtaining a minister's license never crossed my mind. The path unfolded before me as I walked with God. Holding credentials is not a ticket *to* ministry; it is an evidence *of* the ministry already being performed.

most church organizations, credentials allow a minister to voice and vote in local, district, and national elections.

Ordination is an official recognition by a church of a member's call of God to ministry. The church must exercise caution before ordination. In his pastoral letter to Timothy, Paul said, "Lay hands suddenly on no man" (see 1 Tim 5:22). Note the word translated "man" in this verse refers to man, woman, or anyone. What Paul was saying to Timothy was, "Don't be in a hurry to give the sanction of the church." Ordination should not be offered suddenly or considered lightly. An ordained minister acts as a representative of the church investing the credentials in the ministerial candidate. With ordination, comes an identification—a public connection between the church and the person being ordained. It acknowledges the minister holds to the same doctrinal convictions and commitment to the Lord as the church making the investiture.

Debate over the role of women in the church often focuses on whether women should be eligible for ordination. This issue is important because ordination brings with it the opportunity to hold positions of authority. Ordination substantiates the qualification of the ordained indicating he or she is able and authorized to preach, perform religious rites and ceremonies, and/or oversee the administration of a church.

Some have argued that ordination is strictly an Old Testament practice for Jewish priests (see Lev 8). However, in the New Testament, church leaders jointly and publicly acknowledged those called to minister. They anointed them, prayed for them, laid hands on them, and sent them off with their blessings. A modern-day ordination service may not look precisely the same as in the early church, but the intention is equivalent. It validates the ministry already begun by the empowering gift of the spirit of God. The church recognizes those being ordained as qualified to perform certain duties and roles of ministry, activates them, and in so doing protects the church from charlatans, false teachers, or those who might seek to prematurely rise to a position they are not yet ready to fill.

Ordination is precluded by a call of God to separate a certain believer for the work of the gospel. The Holy Spirit spoke and called Paul and Barnabas (see Acts 13:1–4). After the believers in the Antioch church fasted, prayed, and laid hands on them, they sent the men away to minister. The Bible reinforces the concept that God selects his chosen ministers, and this selection is then confirmed by the church (see Acts 13:4). Ordination in a sense, is a divine-human partnership made to further the work of God.

Ordination bestows a delegation of power and includes a vesting of authority. The word *investment* originates with the concept of "putting on vestments" (an investiture) like priests donning their royal robes before ministering before the Lord. The term later came to mean "the act of being invested with an office, right, endowment."[157] Investments are made with hopes for a return—a profit. Investing in women ministers clothes them with authority. Like the garments worn by the priests, it identifies and commissions them to serve as one of the body of believers who ordained them. With ordination, higher positions of service in the church are made accessible to qualified candidates. Other benefits may include tax credits, a housing allowance, and the opportunity to serve as chaplain.

When questioning the ordination of women, a pre-question must be asked: "Does God call women to preach, teach, and function in leadership positions in his church?" If the answer is yes, then the question of ordination should be simple. Ordination is a validation of the call God has placed on men and women to function as apostles, prophets, evangelists, pastors, and teachers. As such, they should be ordained to serve in their calls with all the authority the positions hold regardless of gender.

The only valid case against ordaining women would be a legitimate universal scriptural prohibition. Both the Old and New Testaments record women serving in offices for which men in today's church are ordained. If even one woman functioned as an apostle, prophet, evangelist, pastor, or teacher, a precedent is established. As in a court of law, a precedent is a decision of a proceeding authoritative rule that can be used in the future in similar cases. Precedents found in Scripture were established and set by God's authoritative rule. What the Bible sanctioned in the early church should be allowed in the church today.

Early Catholic Ordination

The practice of ordaining women is longstanding, though not necessarily widely known. *The Apostolic Constitutions* (a collection of early Christian literature [375-380 AD] that offered authoritative directions on church structure)[158] recorded the ordination of deaconesses. Specifically, it said, "Ordain also a deaconess who is faithful and holy, for the ministrations towards women ... the bishop shall anoint her head, as the priests and kings were formerly anointed."[159] It is important to note this practice was allowed in a church that had already adopted a patriarchal order (male headship or control) of the priesthood. Even in this restrictive culture, women were formally ordained into ministry to women.

Some have claimed these deaconesses were the same as the class of widows who were spiritually used in some capacity. However, in this same volume of *The Apostolic Constitutions,* the widows were instructed to be obedient to the deaconesses. These historic documents recognize a deaconess as a separate classification than a widow. In fact, a preference was specified for a deaconess over a widow in assisting clergy.

The Apostolic Constitutions established the ordination procedure for a deaconess. In its preamble it stated the bishop "shalt lay thy hands upon her in the presence of the presbytery."[160] In their presence, he was to offer the following prayer:

"Eternal God ... who didst fill Miriam and Deborah and Hannah and Huldah ... who also in the tabernacle and the temple didst appoint women keepers ... look down now upon this thine handmaid who is designated to the office of deacon ... that she may worthily execute the work instructed to her."[161]

The ceremony of ordination differs in church organizations and has changed over time. Not only the rite has changed, but the qualifications of those being ordained. Men and women in the early church had no Bible school or seminary to attend. They did not have to pass written tests or write theses. This certainly applied in the case of the Twelve apostles as well as other early church leaders including Paul, Timothy, Priscilla and Aquila, and Phebe (see Mark 3:14; John 15:16; Acts 13:2–3, 14:23; Titus 1:5). Education is beneficial, but it was the call of God on men and women chosen by the Lord and ordained by the church to serve.

Conclusion

The Lord designed women to be intelligent, spiritually-led, and fully capable. Without Eve, Eden was "not good." With her, it was complete. Although both Adam and Eve transgressed, God mercifully redeemed his purpose for humanity through the blood of Jesus. Today, all those who are "in Christ" are new creations, born of water and Spirit, one in him.

Throughout the pages of this book, we have seen that God used women in every era to do exploits for his kingdom. In the Old Testament and the New, faithful women prayed, judged, led worship, prophesied, and explained the Word of God. Jesus welcomed female disciples, and Paul affirmed women as his co-laborers able to teach, lead, and operate in the gifts of the Spirit. On the day of Pentecost, the Lord fulfilled his promise and poured out his Spirit on all flesh including his handmaidens or daughters. Since then women have played even greater roles in his kingdom. In revivals over the centuries, wherever the spirit of God moved, women served alongside—and sometimes led—men.

If the issue of women in ministry were straightforward, the church would have united on the subject long ago. Biblical concepts are best understood by balancing views through the "macro lens" of finite human understanding with the "wide angle lens" of the whole counsel of God. In the times our understanding of Scripture is foggy or indeterminate, as sincere believers we cannot pretend it is clear. When a passage's meaning cannot be conclusively determined (as in the case of missing correspondence or one-time word usage), wisdom dictates these verses should not be used to establish universal principles or create what could well be unscriptural barriers.

While biblical teachings and policies are important—especially pertaining to critical issues of salvation and eternal life—we must be careful not to build concrete doctrines on sand. The footings are simply not there to erect a pillar and fasten a Pauline ruling to it that he may not have made or that he did not specify should extend beyond a local situation. Every Christian must examine his or her beliefs against the Word of God and dismiss any augmentation—practices or precepts added along the way that restrict religious freedom.

Accepted interpretations and personal conclusions differ, and Christians should be respectful toward those who have differing beliefs. While we hold to our convictions, we should take care that we are not divisive. Jesus told his followers there would be places their ministry would not be received. In those times, they were to let their peace return to them and "shake off the dust" from their feet as they moved forward in the will of God (see Matt 10:13–14).

Jesus taught his followers that in his kingdom no competition for position or power was ever appropriate. So it should be today. It is in the best interest of the church to have as many passionate, qualified people as possible engaged in ministry. A called woman of God brings a unique benefit to the church. Her contributions in the pulpit and in organizational leadership complement the work of others and strengthen the body of Christ. Providing her a place to minister should not displace another. The kingdom of God is about expansion, not ladder climbing.

It's the Lord's prerogative to allow or disallow women from preaching, pastoring, or leading. In the biblical record we find no instance in which Jesus or other early church leaders restricted women from leadership positions based solely on gender. It seems logical Jesus would have plainly and directly expressed any prohibitions. And he would have transmitted such critical information to those he gave the keys to the kingdom.

Women not only bless the church in pulpit ministry, but their involvement in leadership brings an exciting dynamic to the work of God. Feminine aptitudes, instincts, and gifts are essential components to a healthy church body. In church organizations that license and ordain women, it is appropriate that opportunities should be open for women to serve at varying levels of leadership.

Women serving in ministry is not a part of a progressive liberal agenda, but a historic reality. If there was a Deborah or Huldah in the Old Testament—and a Junia or Priscilla in the New Testament—there can be a Crystal or Lindsay today regardless of male-to-female ratios.

All women are not called to preach, just as all men are not. The question each person must ask and answer is this: "Am I fulfilling the purpose and call of God in my life?"

Women in ministry should be affirmed, equipped, and released to serve. A sister should help a sister, and a true Christian gentleman should hold doors open for the virtuous women of God.

Selected Bibliography

Alexander, Estrelda. *Black Fire: One Hundred Years of African American Pentecostalism,* Downers Grove, IL: IVP Academic, 2011.

Angell, Jeannette L. "Women in the Medievel Church: Did You Know," *Christian History,* Issue 30, 1991, www.christianhistoryinstitute.org/magazine/article/women-in-medieval-church-did-you-know/.

Barfoot, Charles H. and Sheppard, Gerald T. "Prophetic vs. Priestly Religion: The Changing Role of Women Clergy in Classical Pentecostal Churches." *Review of Religious Research,* Vol. 22, No. 1, (Religious Research Association, Inc., 1980), pp. 2-17 Published by: Religious Research Association, Inc. www.jstor.org/stable/3510481.

Bauckham, Richard. *Gospel Women: Studies of the Named Women in the Gospels,* Grand Rapids, MI: Eerdsmans, 2002.

Belleville, Linda L. *Two Views on Women in Ministry,* Revised edition, Grand Rapids, MI: Zondervan, 2005.

Belleville, Linda. *Women Leaders and the Church,* Grand Rapids, MI: Baker, 2000.

Bernard, David K. *The Apostolic Church in the Twenty-first Century,* Hazelwood, MO: Word Aflame Press, 2014.

Booth, Catherine. *Female Ministry, or, Woman's Right to Preach the Gospel,* New York, NY: Salvation Army Supplies Print. and Pub. Dept., 1975, 1859.

Bordin, Ruth. *Frances Willard: A Biography,* Chapel Hill, NC: The University of North Carolina Press, 1986.

Brengle, S. L. *The Soul Winner's Secret,* New York, NY: The Salvation Army Publishing House, New York, 1920.

Burgess, Stanley M., editor. *The New International Dictionary of Pentecostal and Charismatic Movements,* Grand Rapids, MI: Zondervan, 2002.

Butler, Alban. *Butler's Lives of the Saints.* 12 vols. Ed. David Hugh Farmer and Paul Burns. New full ed., Tunbridge Wells, UK: Burns & Oates and Collegeville, MN: Liturgical Press, 1995–2000.

Bullock, Noel. "First Timothy 2:8-15," *McMaster Journal of Theology and Ministry,* Volume 11, Hamilton, Ontario: McMaster Divinity College, 2009-2010.

Coffman, James Burton. "Commentary on 1 Corinthians 1:11," *Coffman Commentaries on the Old and New Testament,* www.studylight.org/commentaries/bcc/1-corinthians-1.html.

Cunningham, Agnes, S.S.C.M., *The Role of Women in Ecclesial Ministry: Biblical and Patristic Roots,* Washington, D.C.: United States Catholic Conference Publications Office, 1976.

Cunningham, Loren, David Joel Hamilton, David Joel, with Rogers, Janice. *Why Not Women?*, Seattle, WA: YWAM Publishing, 2000.

Danby, Herbert, D.D., *The Mishnah: Translated From The Hebrew With Introduction and Brief Explanatory Notes*, New York, NY: Oxford Press, 1933.

Deen, Edith. *All the Woman of the Bible*, San Francisco, CA: HarperOne, 1988.

Donaldson, James (translator). "Apostolic Constitutions," Book III, from *Ante-Nicene Fathers*, Vol. 7. Edited by Alexander Roberts, James Donaldson, and A. Cleveland Coxe, (Buffalo, NY: Christian Literature Publishing Co., 1886.) Revised and edited for New Advent by Kevin Knight. www.newadvent.org/fathers/07153.htm.

Dupont, Florence translated by Hachette, France. *Daily Life in Ancient Rome*. Cambridge, MA: Blackwell Publishers, 1994.

Ellison, Robert H., editor. *A New History of the Sermon: The Nineteenth Century*, Leiden, Netherlands, Boston, MA, Brill, 2010.

Epp, Eldon. *Junia, the First Woman Apostle*. Minneapolis, MN: Augsburg Fortress, 2005.

French, Talmadge L. *Early Interracial Oneness Pentecostalism*, Eugene, OR: Pickwick Publications, 2014.

Gariepy, Henry. *Christianity in Action: The International History of the Salvation Army*, Grand Rapids, MI: Eerdmans Publishing, 2009.

Geller, Stephen A. "The Dynamics of Parallel Verse a Poetic Analysis of Deuteronomy 32:6-12," *The Harvard Theological Review*, Vol. 75, No. 1, Cambridge, MA: Harvard Divinity School, 1982.

Goll, James. *Lifestyle of a Prophet*, Ada, MI: Chosen Books, 2013.

Hallett, Judith P. *Fathers and Daughters in Roman Society: Women and the Elite Family*, Princeton, NJ: Princeton University Press, 1984.

Jeremias, Joachim. *Jerusalem in the Time of Jesus*, Philadelphia, PA: Fortress, 1969.

Kee, H. Clark. *The Origins of Christianity*, London: Prentice-Hall, 1973.

Keener, Craig S. *Paul, Women, and Wives: Marriage and Women's Ministry in the Letters of Paul*, Peabody, MA: Hendrickson Publishers, 1992.

Keener, Craig S. *Two Views on Women in Ministry*, Revised Edition, Grand Rapids, MI: Zondervan, 2005.

Klinedinst, Douglas C. "Spiritual Authority: The Example of the Centurion Servant," *Forward Magazine*, Vol. 47, No. 3, (July – September 2016), 7.

Koren, Daniel J., *He Called Her*, Hazelwood, MO: Word Aflame Press, 2016.

Lange, John Peter, D.D. Translated from German by Schaff, Philip, D.D. *A Commentary on the Holy Scriptures: Critical, Doctrinal, and Homilitical, With Special Reference to Ministers and Students*, Vol. 13., New York, NY: Charles Scribner's Sons, 1876.

Liardon, Roberts (compiler). *Frank Bartleman's Azusa Street: First Hand Accounts of the Revival*, Shippensburg, PA: Destiny Image Publishers, 2006.

Lightfoot, J. B. *St. Paul's Epistle to the Philippians*, London: Macmillan, 1894.

Lockyer, Herbert. *The Women of the Bible*, Grand Rapids, MI: Zondervan, 1988.

McKnight, Scot. *Junia is not Alone*, Englewood, CO: Patheos Press, 2011.

McCray, Gerald. *God's Gals,* Mustang, OK: Tate Publishing, 2004.

McGraw, Barbara A. *The Wiley Blackwell Companion to Religion and Politics in the U.S.,* Chichester, West Sussex: John Wiley & Sons, 2016.

Miller, Cindy. *Character Counts,* Dover, DE: Classic Publishing, 2010.

Murphy-O'Connor, Jerome. *St. Paul's Corinth: Texts and Archeology,* Collegeville, MN: The Liturgical Press, 2002.

Patterson, Eric and Rybarczyk, Edmund. *The Future of Pentecostalism in the United States,* Lanham, MD: Lexington Books, 2007.

Phipps, William E. *Assertive Biblical Women*, WJestport, CT: Greenwood Press, 1992.

Presbuteros, *Reply to a Priest of Rome*, Kensington: J. Wakeham Printer, 1868.

Pugh, J. T. *For Preachers Only,* Hazelwood, MO: Word Aflame Press, 2010.

Ramsay, W. M. "Historical Commentary on the First Epistle to Timothy," *The Expositor*, VIII (September 1909); Walter Lock, "A Critical and Exegetical Commentary on the Pastoral Epistles," *ICC,* Edinburgh: T&T Clark, rep. 1966.

Ramsey, W. M. *The Letters to the Seven Churches of Asia*, London: Hodder and Stoughton, 1904.

Ravenhill, Leonard. *Picture of a Prophet,* ravenhill.org. www.ravenhill.org/prophet.htm.

Scholer, David M. *Women in Early Christian History*, New York & London: Garland Publishing, 1993.

Segraves, Daniel L. "The Battle of the Lexicons: Does 'Head' Refer to Authority or Source?," *Forward Magazine,* Vol. 47, No. 3, July – September 2016, 10.

Spencer, Aida Besançon. *Beyond the Curse,* Nashville, TN: Thomas Nelson, 1985.

Strauch, Alexander. *Biblical Eldership,* Colorado Springs, CO: Lewis and Roth Publishers, 1995.

Sweet, Dr. Leonard. *I Am A Follower*, Nashville, TN: Thomas Nelson, 2012.

Tarn, W. W. and Griffith, G. T., *Hellenistic Civilisation,* 3rd Edition, London: Methuen, 1952.

Trout, Janet. *The Journey of Women in Ministry,* Dover, DE: Classic Publishing, 2009.

Tyson, James L. *The Early Pentecostal Revival,* Hazelwood, MO: Word Aflame Press, 1992.

Walston, Sharon Stoops. *A Woman's Place in God's Government,* House of Loy Books, Wilton, ME, 2001.

Warner, Wayne E. *Neglect Not the Gift That is in Thee*, Metuchen, NJ and London: The Scarecrow Press, Inc., 1986.

Witherington, Ben II and Hyatt, Darlene. *Paul's Letter to the Romans: A Socio-Rhetorical Commentary,* Grand Rapids, MI: Eerdmans, 2004.

Endnotes

Chapter 1

1 Stephen A. Geller, "The Dynamics of Parallel Verse a Poetic Analysis of Deuteronomy 32:6–12," *The Harvard Theological Review*, Vol. 75, No. 1 (Cambridge, MA: Harvard Divinity School, 1982), 35–56.

2 See John 4:24.

3 Strong, *Strong's Exhaustive Concordance of the Bible*, s.v. "help."

4 Strong, *Strong's Exhaustive Concordance of the Bible*, s.v. "meet."

5 Francis Brown, *The Brown-Driver-Briggs Hebrew and English Lexicon* (Peabody, MA: Hendrickson, 2007), 617.

6 *Septuagint*, (Internet Sacred Text Archive), www.sacred-texts.com/bib/sep/gen002.htm.

7 *LSJ*, (Greek Word Study Tool), www.perseus.tufts.edu/hopper/morph?l=%E1%BD%85%CE%BC%CE%BF%CE%B9%CE%BF%CF%82&la=greek, "ὅμοιος."

8 Vine, *Vine's Expository Dictionary of New Testament Words*, s.v. "like."

Chapter 3

9 Wasson, Donald L. "The Extent of the Roman Empire." Ancient History Encyclopedia. Last modified January 05, 2016. http://www.ancient.eu/article/851.

10 David Meager, "Slavery in Bible Times," Crossway Autumn 2006, No. 102, http://archive.churchsociety.org/crossway/documents/Cway_102_Slavery1.pdf.

11 George H. Guthrie, "The Religious Background of the New Testament," Read the Bible for Life Leader Kit, (Lifeway Press: Nashville, TN, 2010).

12 Judith P. Hallett, *Fathers and Daughters in Roman Society: Women and the Elite Family*, (Princeton, NJ: Princeton University Press, 1984). 77-79.

13 Ibid.

14 Mark Cartwright, "Women in Ancient Greece." *Ancient History Encyclopedia*. Last modified July 27, 2016. http://www.ancient.eu/article/927.

15 Demosthenes, Speeches (English), Dem. 59.122, perseus.uchicago.edu/perseus-cgi/citequery3.

pl?dbname=GreekFeb2011&query=Dem.%2059.122&getid=1.

[16] Jerome Murphy-O'Connor, *St. Paul's Corinth: Texts and Archeology*, (Collegeville, MN: The Liturgical Press, 2002), 56.

[17] Jerome Murphy-O'Connor, *St. Paul's Corinth: Texts and Archeology*, 56–57.

[18] Douglas J. Moo (and eight others), *The NIV Application Commentary Bundle 7: Pauline Epistles*, (Grand Rapids, MI: Zondervan, 2015).

[19] Belleville, Linda L, *Two Views on Women in Ministry*, Revised edition, (Grand Rapids, MI: Zondervan, 2005), 45.

[20] Joseph H. Thayer, *Thayer's Greek English Lexicon of the New Testament*, Fourth edition. (Grand Rapids, MI: Baker Book House Company, 1977), s.v. "evangelist."

[21] Ibid.

[22] Herbert Lockyer, *The Women of the Bible*, (Grand Rapids, MI: Zondervan, 1988). www.biblegateway.com/resources/all-women-bible/New-Testament-Times. 11 Feb. 2017.

[23] Ibid.

[24] Ibid.

[25] Vine, *Vine's Expository Dictionary of New Testament Words*, s.v. "disciple."

[26] Joachim Jeremias, *Jerusalem in the Time of Jesus*, (Philadelphia, PA: Fortress, 1969), 375–76.

Chapter 4

[27] Strong, *Strong's Exhaustive Concordance of the Bible,* s.v. "assemble."

[28] Edith Deen, *All the Woman of the Bible*, (San Francisco, CA: HarperOne, 1988), 357.

[29] John Peter Lange, D.D., Translated from German by Philip Schaff, D.D, *A Commentary on the Holy Scriptures: Critical, Doctrinal, and Homilitical, With Special Reference to Ministers and Students*, Vol. 13., (New York, NY: Charles Scribner's Sons, 1876), 145.

[30] Ibid.

[31] H. W. F. Gesenius, Transcribed by Samuel Prideaux Tregelles, *Gesenius' Hebrew and Chaldee Lexicon to the Old Testament Scriptures*, 7th edition, (Grand Rapids, MI: Baker Book House; 1979), s.v. "Miriam."

[32] Paul Isaac Hershon (Compiler and Translator), *Talmudic Miscellany*, (London: Trubner & Company, 1880,) 283.

[33] Walter Brueggemann, *First and Second Samuel*, (Louisville, KY: John Knox, 1990), 21.

[34] Judy Bolton-Fasman, "Hannah's Prayer: A Rosh Hashanah Story," *Jewish Boston* (2016). www.jewishboston.com/hannahs-prayer-a-rosh-hashanah-story/.

[35] Paulus Cassell, D.D., *Lange's Commentary: The Book of Judges*, (New York, NY: Charles Scribner and Company, 1872), 105.

[36] William E. Phipps, *Assertive Biblical Women*, (Westport, CT: Greenwood Press, 1992), 85.

Chapter 5

[37] Strong, *Strong's Exhaustive Concordance of the Bible*, s.v. "disciple."

[38] Ibid.

[39] Rev. Kevin M. Shaw, Personal interview, 19 Nov. 2016.

[40] Eusebius of Caesarea, *Fathers of the Church*, Book 3. Chapter 31. www.newadvent.org/fathers/250103.htm.

[41] Strong, *Strong's Exhaustive Concordance of the Bible*, s.v. "kyrios."

[42] Ibid.

[43] Robert Law, "Elect Lady," *International Standard Bible Encyclopedia*, www.blueletterbible.org/search/dictionary/viewTopic.cfm?topic=ET0001150,IT0002949.

[44] Ibid.

[45] Eusebius. *An Ecclesiastical History to the Twentieth Year of the Reign of Constantine, being the 324th of the Christian Era*, (London: S. Bagster, 1842), 141.

[46] Strong, *Strong's Exhaustive Concordance of the Bible*, s.v. "abide."

[47] W. W. Tarn and G. T. Griffith, *Hellenistic Civilisation*, 3rd Edition, (London: Methuen, 1952), 98–9.

[48] Ibid.

[49] W.M. Ramsey, *The Letters to the Seven Churches of Asia*, (London: Hodder and Stoughton, 1904), 324–35.

[50] Coffman, James Burton. "Commentary on 1 Corinthians 1:11," *Coffman Commentaries on the Old and New Testament*, www.studylight.org/commentaries/bcc/1-corinthians-1.html.

[51] Donald S. Metz, *Beacon Bible Commentary*, VIII, (Kansas City, KA: Beacon Hill Press, 1968), 314.

[52] John Trap, "Commentary on 1 Corinthians 1:11," *John Trapp Complete Commentary*, www.studylight.org/commentaries/jtc/1-corinthians-1.html.

[53] Daniel Whedon, "Commentary on 1 Corinthians 1:11," *Whedon's Commentary on the Bible*, www.studylight.org/commentaries/whe/1-corinthians-1.html.

[54] John Gill, "Commentary on 1 Corinthians 1:11," *The New John Gill Exposition of the Entire Bible*, www.studylight.org/commentaries/geb/1-corinthians-1.html.

[55] Florence Dupont translated by France Hachette, *Daily Life in Ancient Rome*. (Cambridge, MA: Blackwell Publishers, 1994), 103–5.

[56] T. Hammer, "Wealthy Widows and Female Apostles: The Economic and Social Status of Women in Early Roman Christianity," in G. D. Dunn, D. Luckensmeyer & L. Cross (ed.), *Prayer and Spirituality in the Early Church: Poverty and Riches*, 5 (Strathfield: Paulist Press, 2009), 65–74.

[57] Richard S. Cervin, "A Note Regarding the Name 'Junia(s)' in Romans 16:7," *New Testament Studies*, Volume 40.3 (Cambridge, MA: Cambridge University Press, 1994), 464–470.

[58] Eldon Epp, *Junia, the First Woman Apostle*. (Minneapolis, MN: Augsburg Fortress, 2005).

[59] John Chrysostom, *Homily on the Epistle of St. Paul the Apostle to the Romans XXXI*, (Oxford/London: John Henry Parker/J. Rivington, 1848), 489.

[60] Epp, *Junia, the First Woman Apostle*, 34

[61] David Noel Freedman, ed., *The Anchor Bible Dictionary*, (New York, NY: Doubleday, 1992), 1127.

[62] James R. Beck, editor, Craig S. Keener, *Two Views on Women in Ministry*, Revised Edition, (Grand Rapids, MI: Zondervan, 2005), 212–13.

[63] Strong, *Strong's Exhaustive Concordance of the Bible*, s.v. "en."

[64] Thayer, *Thayer's Greek English Lexicon of the New Testament*, s.v. "among."

[65] Ben Witherington II and Darlene Hyatt, *Paul's Letter to the Romans: A Socio-Rhetorical Commentary*, (Grand Rapids, MI: Eerdmans, 2004), 389.

[66] Scot McKnight, *Junia is not Alone*, (Englewood, CO: Patheos Press, 2011), Kindle Locations 73–75.

[67] Richard Bauckham, *Gospel Women: Studies of the Named Women in the Gospels*, (Grand Rapids, MI: Eerdsmans, 2002), 109–202.

[68] Strong, *Strong's Exhaustive Concordance of the Bible*, s.v. "diakonos."

[69] Edith Deen, *All the Woman of the Bible*, (San Francisco, CA: HarperOne, 1988), 231.

[70] Strong, *Strong's Exhaustive Concordance of the Bible*, s.v. "prostates."

[71] Aida Besançon Spencer, *Beyond the Curse*, (Nashville, TN: Thomas Nelson, 1985), 116–17.

[72] Strong, *Strong's Exhaustive Concordance of the Bible*, s.v. "proïstēmi."

[73] Booth, *Female Ministry, or, Woman's Right to Preach the Gospel*, 11.

Chapter 6

[74] Loren Cunningham, David Joel Hamilton, with Janice Rogers, *Why Not Women?*, (Seattle, WA: YWAM Publishing, 2000), 13.

[75] Ibid.

[76] Daniel L. Segraves, "The Battle of the Lexicons: Does 'Head' Refer to Authority or Source?," *Forward Magazine*, Vol. 47, No. 3, July – September 2016, 10.

[77] Ibid.

[78] Thayer, *Thayer's Greek English Lexicon of the New Testament*, s.v. "strong."

[79] Booth, *Female Ministry, or, Woman's Right to Preach the Gospel*, 8.

[80] Ibid.

[81] Catherine Booth, *Female Ministry, or, Woman's Right to Preach the Gospel*, 9.

[82] Spencer, *Beyond the Curse*.

[83] Herbert Danby, D.D., *The Mishnah: Translated From The Hebrew With Introduction and Brief Explanatory Notes* (New York, NY: Oxford Press, 1933), 447.

[84] *The Greek New Testament*, Third Edition, United Bible Societies (New York, London, Amsterdam, Edinburgh, Stuttgart, 1975), www.greekbible.com/l.php?manqa/nw_v-3pad-s--.

[85] Interlinear Study Bible, classic.studylight.org/desk/view.cgi?number=5720&tool=grk.

[86] Cunningham, *Why Not Women, A Fresh Look at Scripture on Women in Missions*, Ministry and Leadership, 218.

87 Spencer, *Beyond the Curse* (Grand Rapids, MI: Baker Academic, 1985).

88 Vine, *Vine's Expository Dictionary of New Testament Words*, s.v. "silence."

89 Alexandrinus Philo, *Philo, Volume 2*, (Cambridge, MA: Harvard University Press, 1979), 131.

90 William E. Wenstrom, Jr., *De*, Wenstrom Bible Ministries, wenstrom.org/downloads/written/word_studies/greek/de.pdf.

91 Vine, *Vine's Expository Dictionary of New Testament Words*, s.v. "authority."

92 Ibid.

93 Noel Bullock, "First Timothy 2:8–15," *McMaster Journal of Theology and Ministry*, Volume 11, (Hamilton, Ontario: McMaster Divinity College, 2009–2010), 81.

94 Ibid.

95 Gerald McCray, *God's Gals*, (Mustang, OK: Tate Publishing, 2004), 39.

96 Ibid.

97 Ibid.

98 S. L. Brengle, *The Soul Winner's Secret,* (New York, NY: The Salvation Army Publishing House, New York, 1920), 36.

99 Linda L. Belleville, *Women Leaders and the Church*, (Grand Rapids, MI: Baker, 2000), 165.

100 W. M. Ramsay, "Historical Commentary on the First Epistle to Timothy," *The Expositor*, VIII (September 1909); Walter Lock, "A Critical and Exegetical Commentary on the Pastoral Epistles," ICC (Edinburgh: T&T Clark, rep. 1966), 31.

101 Booth, *Female Ministry, or, Woman's Right to Preach the Gospel*, 13.

102 Ibid.

Chapter 7

103 Jeannette L. Angell, "Women in the Medievel Church: Did You Know," *Christian History*, Issue 30, 1991, www.christianhistoryinstitute.org/magazine/article/women-in-medieval-church-did-you-know/.

104 Ibid.

105 H. Clark Kee, *The Origins of Christianity*, (London: Prentice-Hall, 1973), 51-2.

106 Joyce Ellen Salisbury, "Perpetua," *Encyclopedia Britannica*. (10 Nov. 1999), www.britannica.com/biography/Perpetua-Christian-martyr.

107 Eusebius of Caesarea, *340 AD Church History*: Book 6, Chapter 41. www.documentacatholicaomnia.eu/03d/0265-0339,_Eusebius_Caesariensis,_Church_History,_EN.pdf.

108 Johann Peter Kirsch, "St. Apollonia," *The Catholic Encyclopedia*, Vol. 1. (New York, NY: Robert Appleton Company, 1907).

109 Ibid.

110 Clugnet, Léon Clugnet, "St. Catherine of Alexandria." *The Catholic Encyclopedia*. Vol. 3, (New York, NY: Robert Appleton Company, 1908), Newadvent.org.

111 David M. Scholer, *Women in Early Christian History,* (New York & London: Garland Publishing, 1993), 310.

112 Alban Butler, Butler's *Lives of the Saints.* 12 vols. Ed. David Hugh Farmer and Paul Burns. New full ed., (Tunbridge Wells, UK: Burns & Oates and Collegeville, MN: Liturgical Press, 1995–2000).

113 Belleville, *Two Views on Women in Ministry*, 46.

114 Ibid., 45.

115 Strong, *Strong's Exhaustive Concordance of the Bible*, s.v. "elder."

116 Alexander Strauch, *Biblical Eldership*, (Colorado Springs, CO: Lewis and Roth Publishers, 1995), 16.

117 J. B. Lightfoot, *St. Paul's Epistle to the Philippians.* (London: Macmillan, 1894), 95.

118 J. Mark Jordan, "Abuse of Spiritual Authority," *Forward Magazine*, Vol. 47, No. 3, (July –September 2016), 15.

119 Strong, *Strong's Exhaustive Concordance of the Bible*, s.v. "diakoneō."

120 Philip Comfort, General Editor, *Cornerstone Biblical Commentary*, (Carol Stream, IL: Tyndale House Publishers, 2009), 75.

121 Charles John Ellicott, General Editor, *Ellicott's Commentary for English Readers*, (London, Paris, New York and Melbourne: Cassell and Company, Ltd., 1905). biblehub.com/commentaries/ellicott/1_timothy/3.htm.

122 Ibid.

123 Ellicott, *Ellicott's Commentary for English Readers.*

124 Agnes Cunningham, S.S.C.M., *The Role of Women in Ecclesial Ministry: Biblical and Patristic Roots*, (Washington, D.C.: United States Catholic Conference Publications Office, 1976).

125 Ibid.

126 Ibid.

127 Douglas C. Klinedinst, "Spiritual Authority: The Example of the Centurion Servant," *Forward Magazine*, Vol. 47, No. 3, (July – September 2016), 7.

Chapter 8

128 "Phoebe Palmer: Mother of the Holiness Movement," *Christianity Today*, www.christianitytoday.com/history/people/moversandshakers/phoebe-palmer.html.

129 Ruth Bordin, *Frances Willard: A Biography*, (Chapel Hill, NC: The University of North Carolina Press, 1986), 87.

130 Barbara A McGraw, *The Wiley Blackwell Companion to Religion and Politics in the U.S.*, (Chichester, West Sussex: John Wiley & Sons, 2016), 179.

131 Frances E Willard. (1890). "A White Life for Two." *Illinois During the Guilded Age*, www.gildedage.lib.niu.edu/islandora/object/niu-gildedage%3A24224.

132 Editors of the Encyclopedia Britannica, "Hannah Whitehall-Smith: American Evangelist and Reformer." *The Encyclopedia Britannica*, www.britannica.com/biography/Hannah-Whitall-Smith.

133 Robert H. Ellison, editor, *A New History of the Sermon: The Nineteenth Century*, (Leiden, Netherlands, Boston, MA, Brill, 2010), 395.

134 Norman H. Murcoch, "The Army Mother," *Christian History Institute*. www.christianhistoryinstitute. org/magazine/article/army-mother/.

135 Henry Gariepy, *Christianity in Action: The International History of the Salvation Army*, (Grand Rapids, MI: Eerdmans Publishing, 2009), 36.

136 James Goll, *Lifestyle of a Prophet*, (Ada, MI: Chosen Books, 2013), 232–3.

137 Ibid.

138 James L. Tyson, *The Early Pentecostal Revival*, (Hazelwood, MO: Word Aflame Press, 1992), 36

139 Tyson, *The Early Pentecostal Revival*, 45.

140 Marshall Allen, "Pentecostal Movement Celebrates Humble Roots," (15 Apr 2006), *The Washington Post*, www.washingtonpost.com/wp-dyn/content/article/2006/04/14/AR2006041401421.html. Retrieved 26 Nov. 2016).

141 Roberts Liardon (compiler), *Frank Bartleman's Azusa Street: First Hand Accounts of the Revival*. (Shippensburg, PA: Destiny Image Publishers, 2006), 57.

142 Stanley M. Burgess, editor, *The New International Dictionary of Pentecostal and Charismatic Movements*, (Grand Rapids, MI: Zondervan, 2002), 588.

143 Tyson, *The Early Pentecostal Revival*, 151.

144 Talmadge L. French, *Early Interracial Oneness Pentecostalism*, (Eugene, OR: Pickwick Publications, 2014), 67.

145 Wayne E. Warner, *Neglect Not the Gift That is in Thee*, (Metuchen, NJ and London: The Scarecrow Press, Inc., 1986), 146.

146 "Aimee Semple McPherson," *Christian History*, ChristianityToday.com. www.christianitytoday.com/ history/people/denominationalfounders/aimee-semple-mcpherson.html. Accessed 24 Mar. 2016.

147 Estrelda Alexander, *Black Fire: One Hundred Years of African American Pentecostalism*, (Downers Grove, IL: IVP Academic, 2011), 329.

148 "History," International Christian Education Association of the Pentecostal Assemblies of the World. pawicea.org/about/history/.

149 Charles H. Barfoot and Gerald T. Sheppard, "Prophetic vs. Priestly Religion: The Changing Role of Women Clergy in Classical Pentecostal Churches." *Review of Religious Research*, Vol. 22, No. 1, (Religious Research Association, Inc., 1980), pp. 2–17 Published by: Religious Research Association, Inc. www.jstor.org/stable/3510481.

150 Liardon, *Frank Bartleman's Azusa Street: First Hand Accounts of the Revival*, 57.

151 Eric Patterson and Edmund Rybarczyk, *The Future of Pentecostalism in the United States*, (Lanham, MD: Lexington Books, 2007), 128–9.

152 Ibid.

153 Ibid.

Chapter 9

[154] Pugh, *For Preachers Only*, 87.

[155] Sharon Stoops Walston, *A Woman's Place in God's Government*, (House of Loy Books, Wilton, ME 2001).

[156] David K. Bernard, *The Apostolic Church in the Twenty-first Century*, (Hazelwood, MO: Word Aflame Press, 2014), 87.

[157] Investment, Dictionary.com, *Dictionary.com Unabridged*, (Random House), www.dictionary.com/browse/investment.

[158] James Donaldson (translator), "Apostolic Constitutions," Book III, from *Ante-Nicene Fathers*, Vol. 7. Edited by Alexander Roberts, James Donaldson, and A. Cleveland Coxe, (Buffalo, NY: Christian Literature Publishing Co., 1886.) Revised and edited for New Advent by Kevin Knight. www.newadvent.org/fathers/07153.htm.

[159] Ibid.

[160] Roberts and Donaldson, *Ante-Nicene Fathers*, Vol. 7, (Grand Rapids, MI: Eerdmans Publishing Company, 1988), 492.

[161] Ibid.

CPSIA information can be obtained
at www.ICGtesting.com
Printed in the USA
FFHW01n1230090718
47363201-50453FF